THE COURAGE TO LOVE

THE COURAGE TO LOVE

PRINCIPLES AND PRACTICES OF SELF-RELATIONS PSYCHOTHERAPY

Stephen Gilligan, Ph.D.

W.W. Norton & Company   New York   London

The author wishes to acknowledge publishers of earlier versions of some of the material in this book: Chapter 1 is based on "When I Sit with a Client," *Journal of Systemic Therapies*, in press; parts of Chapters 3 and 6 appeared in "The Relational Self: The Expanding of Love beyond Desire," *Constructive Therapies, Volume 2*, edited by Michael Hoyt, New York: Guilford, 1996; a section of Chapter 7 appeared in "The Fight against Fundamentalism: Searching for Soul in Erickson's Legacy," *Ericksonian Methods: The Essence of the Story*, edited by Jeffrey K. Zeig, New York: Brunner/Mazel, 1996; Chapter 8 is based on "Therapeutic Rituals," *Therapeutic Conversations*, edited by Stephen Gilligan and Reese Price, New York: Norton, 1993.

Other credits: Excerpts from two poems appearing in Anthony Machado's *Times Alone: Selected Poems of Antonio Machado* © 1983 Wesleyan University Press by permission of University Press of New England. Reprinted with the permission of Simon & Schuster from *The Collected Works of W. B. Yeats, Volume 1: The Poems*, revised and edited by Richard J. Finneran. Copyright © 1924 by Macmillan Publishing Company, renewed 1952 by Bertha Georgie Yeats. Reprinted with the permission of A. P. Watt Ltd. on behalf of Michael Yeats. A version of Kavanah (a Jewish reading of intentionality) by Rabbi Michael Strassfeld from *The New Jewish Catalog*, Schoken Books, forthcoming. From *The Prophet* by Kahlil Gibran. Copyright 1923 by Kahlil Gibran and renewed 1951 by Administrators CTA of Kahlil Gibran estate and Mary G. Gibran. Reprinted by permission of Alfred A. Knopf., Inc. "The Good Silence," from *Loving a Woman in Two Worlds* by Robert Bly. Copyright © 1985 by Robert Bly. Used by permission of Doubleday, a division of Bantam Doubleday Dell Publishing Group, Inc. "Four Ways of Knowledge," from *The Man in the Black Coat Turns* by Robert Bly. Copyright © 1981 by Robert Bly. Used by permission of Doubleday, a division of Bantam Doubleday Dell Publishing Group, Inc. Excerpt from "Keeping Quiet" from *Extravagaria* by Pablo Neruda, translated by Alastair Reid. Translation copyright © 1974 by Alastair Reid. Reprinted by permission of Farrar, Straus & Giroux, Inc. Excerpts from pages 101, 105 as submitted from *Selected Poems of Rainer Maria Rilke*, Edited and Translated by Robert Bly. Copyright © 1981 by Robert Bly.

Copyright (c) 1997 by Stephen Gilligan

For information about permission to reproduce selections from this book, write to Permissions, W. W. Norton & Company, Inc., 500 Fifth Avenue, New York, NY 10110.

Composition by Eastern Composition
Manufacturing by Haddon Craftsmen

Library of Congress Cataloging-in-Publication Data
Gilligan, Stephen G., 1954–
    The courage to love : principles and practices of self-relations
psychotherapy / Stephen Gilligan.
        p.   cm.
    "A Norton professional book"—Prelim. p.
    Includes bibliographical references and index.
    ISBN 0-393-70247-2
    1. Self.   2. Psychotherapy.   3. Love.   I. Title.
RC489.S43G55   1997
616.89'14—dc21   97-467   CIP

W. W. Norton & Company, Inc., 500 Fifth Avenue, New York, N.Y. 10110
                    http://www.wwnorton.com
W. W. Norton & Company Ltd., 10 Coptic Street, London WC1A 1PU

1   2   3   4   5   6   7   8   9   0

To my mother,
Catherine Gilligan,
for all the courage to love
she has encouraged and inspired

CONTENTS

ACKNOWLEDGMENTS

MANY PEOPLE have helped me in the writing of this book. My parents, Cathy and Jack Gilligan, showed me the power of love. My wife, Denise, and my daughter, Zoe, have touched me with its healing force and given me opportunities to develop the capacity to give and receive love. To all of them I am forever grateful.

My main mentors include my mother, Milton Erickson, Gregory Bateson, Gordon Bower, and my aikido sensei, Coryl Crane. Each of these superb and devoted teachers has helped me immensely, at both technical and personal levels.

I am also indebted to all of the clients with whom I have worked. It is a privilege and joy to experience a person's courage and commitment in learning to love self and other, especially when some parts of life suggest that it may be a naive, impossible, or dangerous thing to do.

My teaching (and hence learning) has been supported by many workshop sponsors, including Marilyn Atkinson; Steve Beck; Jack Bloom; Bill Becket, David Stern, and Laine Gifford; Seyma Calihman; Eileen Caulley; Sam Cangelosi; Jeff and Cheryl Chang; Robert Dilts, Judith deLozier, and Teresa Epstein; Jeff Zeig and the Erickson Foundation; Barbara Fairfield; Carol Fitzsimons, Irene Michon and Carl Allen Tippins; Lusijah Marx, Jane Parsons and NYSEPH; Julian Russel; Gunther Schmidt; Bob and Kim Schwarz; Robert Weisz; and Michael Yapko.

Special appreciation goes to the members of the ongoing supervision groups in Austin, Connecticut, Encinitas, New York City, the Oregon coast, Washington state, and West Virginia, and the Boston "Bean" group. Also to friends and colleagues, including Jack Bloom, Robert Dilts, Yvonne Dolan and Charlie Johnson, Carol Fitzimmons, Bill O'Hanlon, Maureen O'Hara, Gunther Schmidt, Harry Shifman, Dvorah Simon, and Jeffrey Zeig.

My dear friend, Barry Elkin, has been with me through many highs and lows, his support unwavering and his love inspiring.

The peer support groups that have nurtured my development include the long-running couples group and the Solana Beach relational studies group.

My editor, Susan Munro, has been remarkably patient and gently instructive in guiding the manuscript to publication.

To these people and many more, thank you.

INTRODUCTION

Queen Malika, wife of the King of Kosala, was one of the first lady converts (to Buddhism). The king wasn't a Buddhist, but he loved her very much. One day on the full moon night, they were very romantic—you know, Buddhism is very romantic—and the king asked her, "My dear, who do you love most?", expecting that she would say, "Of course, your majesty, I love you most."

But being Buddhist she said, "You know, dear, I love *myself* most." And the king said, "Yes, come to think of it, I *also* love myself most."

The next day they went to see the Buddha, and the Buddha said, "Every being loves herself or himself most. If you love yourself best, understand other beings also love themselves best. And the best way to love yourself is not to exploit yourself. If you cultivate greed, hate and delusion, you exploit yourself most."

I think perhaps in the West they could learn a bit of that. I feel people have a lot of hatred for themselves. Loving yourself is the first step to freedom.

The next step, the Buddha said to the king and queen, was not to feel that you are superior to others. For me, that is part of freedom. If you practice the feeling of not feeling superior to others, then you must also practice not to feel *inferior* to others. And ultimately you are taught not to feel *equal* to others. Then you can go beyond dualism, and once you go beyond dualism, interbeing is possible. And that is real freedom: freedom above dualism, beyond you and me, beyond I and thou.

—Sulak Sivaraska, in Sivaraska & Harding, 1995, p. 61

THIS IS A BOOK about how psychotherapy may be used to cultivate the courage and freedom to love. It is written in a time when
love seems to be fading and hatred and despair rising, when community is forgotten and only differences remain. It sees love as a
skill and a force that can heal and invigorate, reconnect and
guide, calm and encourage.

The Jungian therapist Marion Woodman (1993) has suggested
that the main idea of our atomic era is the releasing of energy
from matter. This idea echoes the old Hassidic notion that good
actions release the "sparks of light" that permeate every person,
place, and thing. In this same sense, psychotherapy seeks to liberate the energy, resources, and potentialities implicit in each person. It seeks to water the seeds of self-love and confidence, so
that old limitations fall away and new possibilities bloom.

Central to this task is the skill of love. To use it effectively, we
must understand its nature. As Erich Fromm (1956) commented,
we must supplant sentimental and passive ideas of love with
more active, radical ones. Curiously, love is often seen as something that happens to you in positive circumstances, a drug-like
state that dampens your capacity to act clearly and soberly. Carried further, the idea of "loving one's enemy," or using love effectively in difficult or even violent circumstances, is seen at best as
an unsophisticated understanding held by well-intentioned people
(such as Jesus, Gandhi, M. L. King, or Nelson Mandela) who
really don't know the "real" world. Seen in these frames, love is
irrelevant, even unethical and dangerous, to the psychotherapist.

This book suggests more practical ideas of love and examines
how they may be helpful in psychotherapy. Love is seen as both a
force and a skill involving the relational abilities to protect and
not manipulate life, to give and receive, to be and be with, to
harmonize and differentiate, to touch and liberate. It is a presence
that underlies the effective use of our methods and techniques.
When it's there, our actions and thinking are more tuned, more
flexible, more helpful; when it's not, psychotherapy often becomes a further manipulation and exploitation of the client.

Ideas of love seem especially important in our television-
driven, computer-speed postmodern time, with its cacophony of
ever-increasing images, viewpoints, and descriptions. Lost in this
whirlwind of mental channel-surfing is the wisdom of the body,

the rhythms of nature, the spaces in between, and the community of the human experience. With this loss, differences are threats calling for further battles, more dominance-submission strategies, a further Balkanization of consciousness. It is no wonder that we have difficulties getting along, with both ourselves and others.

In therapy, we see on a daily basis the posttraumatic effects of these intrapsychic and interpersonal battles. We see the despair, the depressions, the addictions, the compulsive violence against self and others, the unremitting anxieties. We see a world where love is increasingly absent, hatred more dominant, and fear more pervasive. In our own small ways, we must try to rekindle the sparks of self-love, to invite acceptance and curiosity where rejection and control have been, to encourage a reawakening of self-in-community. Love is seen as the skill by which this shift in consciousness and relatedness may be navigated.

Clearly, the practice of love has many paths. This book examines the self-relations approach to psychotherapy as one such path. I developed self-relations psychotherapy over the past twenty years of clinical practice and teaching. My early mentors were Milton Erickson and Gregory Bateson. Later influences have included the martial art of aikido; the work of Gandhi, King and others in nonviolent resistance; Buddhist writers, including Pema Chodron and Thich Nhat Hanh; various other writers, including Robert Bly, Erich Fromm, and Carl Jung; and my wife Denise and daughter Zoe. Its most direct contributors have been the many students, clients, and colleagues who have informed me over the years.

The book is organized into three parts. Part I presents the general theoretical and ethical principles of self-relations psychotherapy. Chapter 1 describes six basic premises: (1) you are born with an indestructible "soft spot" or center; (2) life moves through you, except when it doesn't; (3) life is wonderful, but sometimes it hurts like hell; (4) there are two of you (that is, you are relationship); (5) an intelligence greater than you exists in the world; and (6) your way is unique. These ideas provide a basis for both therapist and client to view problems and symptoms in a favorable light. Especially important is the idea of sponsorship of experience, which states that without a mature human presence, experiences will have no human value.

Chapter 2 explores the question of how we deal with relational differences—for example, the difference between my truth and yours, where I want to be and where I am, what you think and what you feel. Self-relations sees this question as primary to the nature and quality of psychological experience, especially in terms of how the "other" (self, truth, person) is regarded and treated. Three distinct approaches to relational differences—fundamentalism, consumerism and love—are detailed, especially in terms of their attentional style. We will see how holding attention too tight gives rise to the paranoid fury and fear of fundamentalism, where the other is to be hated and destroyed. Holding too loose, we drift into the wastelands of consumerism, where indifference and addiction pervade. Holding "not too tight, not too loose," the relational empathy of love is possible. Love is a spirit-based, more fluid approach to experience that emphasizes relationship between multiple views and truths. It relies on the ethical coherence and creativity of nonviolent approaches, especially in violent circumstances, to generate solutions to painful dilemmas or symptoms. As we will see, it requires great courage, rigor, commitment, and tenderness.

Chapter 3 lays out the formal premises of a relational self. Three characteristics are emphasized: (1) a beingness of consciousness; (2) a belongingness to a field; and (3) a relatedness to others. When these characteristics are active, a person's experience is fed by three sources: (1) a somatic self that lives in the body, connected to the river of life and all its archetypal patterns, feelings, and experiences; (2) a cognitive self based in the head and making meanings, plans, social understandings, and other intellectual formulations; and (3) an intelligent relational field to which a person belongs. Symptoms are described as persistent "breaks" in beingness, belongingness, and relatedness that create separateness and opposition between the three sources. The chapter suggests how psychotherapy may identify and repair these breaks, and restore harmony among the different aspects of the relational self.

Part II describes basic practices for putting these principles into relational action. Chapter 4 outlines some technical ways that attention may be shifted in both therapist and client, allowing a more centered and effective responsiveness. Therapy and life itself are approached as performance arts requiring attentiveness to how relatedness within and between persons is developed, maintained, and expressed. Specific methods are detailed for reorganizing attention from fixation to text-based theories (the way things "should be") to process- and field-based expressions (connection and responsiveness to the way things are).

Chapter 5 examines love as a practice or skill, focusing especially on how it may be used under adversarial or difficult circumstances. A prototype exercise regarding self as the relational connection weaving multiple identities is first presented. Therapeutic skills of sponsorship of experience are then examined. Finally, a modified practice of tonglen, a Tibetan method for transforming negative experiences, is presented.

Part III outlines three different therapy methods that use these principles and practices of self-relations to help clients in stuck situations. Chapter 6 outlines the basic prototype of self-relations psychotherapy. Specific descriptions of the identified problem reveal three difficulties: (1) the cognitive self is dissociated or otherwise disconnected; (2) the somatic self is "neglected" and "out of control"; and (3) negative sponsors are attacking with self-alienating ideas. Self-relations thus works to reactivate and maintain the presence and competencies of the cognitive self, accept and integrate the neglected experiences of the somatic self, and identify and differentiate from negative sponsors.

Chapter 7 examines the relevance of archetypal process to psychotherapy. Elaborating on the earlier idea that life moves through you, we will see how life requires that we develop certain skills and how each way of being is represented by an archetypal tradition. For example, learning to love and become part of something bigger than ourselves is connected to the Lover archetype. Learning to differentiate, make and keep specific commitments, and maintain specific boundaries is embodied by the Warrior archetype. Transforming identity, healing wounds, and shifting frames describes aspects of the Magician/Healer tradition. And providing "blessings" and place for each and every aspect of life, internal and external, is the task of the King/Queen archetype. We will see that each archetype has many possible expressions, some positive and some negative, and how skills of sponsorship, love, and other self-relations principles can be used to transform negative expressions into positive ones.

The final chapter examines the method of therapeutic rituals.

Symptoms are seen as partly archetypal events arising at times of identity transitions in a person's life. Without some cultural context for receiving and guiding these energies, suffering and confusion are likely to develop. In this sense, symptoms are seen as attempts for ritual change without a ritual container. The chapter explores how therapy might provide a container that holds, blesses, guides, and encourages the positive transformation of archetypal energies.

Throughout the book, psychotherapy is regarded as a rigorous poetic practice rather than a literal scientific truth. Allan Ginsberg (1992) has described the poetic approach in the following way:

> Real poetry practitioners are practitioners of mind awareness, or practitioners of reality, expressing their fascination with a phenomenal universe and trying to penetrate to the heart of it. Poetics isn't mere picturesque dilettantism or egotistical expressionism for craven motives grasping for sensation and flattery. Classical poetry is a "process," or experiment—a probe into the nature of reality and the nature of the mind.
>
> . . . You need a certain deconditioning of attitude—a deconditioning of rigidity and unyieldingness—so that you can get to the heart of your own thought. That's parallel with traditional Buddhist ideas of renunciation—renunciation of hand-me-down conditioned conceptions of mind. . . . it requires cultivation of tolerance toward one's own thoughts and impulses and ideas—the tolerance necessary for the perception of one's own mind, the kindness to the self necessary for acceptance of that process of consciousness and for acceptance of the mind's raw contents. (pp. 99–100)

A major goal of a poetic approach is to reconnect language with felt experience, and to liberate meaning from fixed assumptions. This is the goal of self-relations work. The interest is in examining practices that cultivate a relational self, one that holds differences and creates harmonies. The hope is that it will encourage the rigor of a heart-based discipline, rather than the tyranny and disappointment of a dogma-based approach. May you read the book as a poem to awaken your self and others!

There is hardly any word which is more ambiguous and confusing than the word "love." It is used to denote almost every feeling short of hate and disgust. It comprises everything from the love for ice cream to the love for a symphony, from mild sympathy to the most intense feeling of closeness. People feel they love if they have "fallen for" somebody. They call their dependence love, and their possessiveness too. They believe, in fact, that nothing is easier than to love, that the difficulty lies in finding the right object, and that their failure to find happiness in love is due to their bad luck in not finding the right partner. But contrary to all this confused and wishful thinking, love is a very specific feeling; and while every human being has a capacity for love, its realization is one of the most difficult achievements.

—*Erich Fromm, 1947, p. 13*

I

PRINCIPLES

1

A River Runs through It

BASIC PREMISES OF THE RELATIONAL SELF

The center I cannot find
Is known to my unconscious mind.

—*W. H. Auden*

Human beings are discourse. The flowing moves through you
whether you say anything or not. Everything that happens is
filled with pleasure and warmth because of the delight of the
discourse that's always going on.

—*J. Rumi, in Barks, 1995*

EVERY THERAPY is guided by ideas about how life works and
doesn't work. Such principles are often implicit, weaving (and
woven into) the multilayered fabric of a therapy conversation.
We begin our discussion of self-relations with six ideas that move
through what Bateson (in Keeney, 1977, p. 49) called "the weave
of the total complex." Listed in Table 1.1, these premises provide
a way of thinking, a way of perceiving, a way of experiencing
both therapist and client, and a way of acting.

TABLE 1.1. BASIC PREMISES OF SELF-RELATIONS THERAPY

1. An indestructible "tender soft spot" exists at the core of each person.
2. Life moves through you, except when it doesn't.
3. Life is great, but sometimes it hurts like hell.
4. There are two of you: Relationship is the basic unit.
5. An intelligence greater than you exists in the world.
6. Your path is yours alone: You are an incurable deviant.

Premise 1: An indestructible "tender soft spot" exists at the core of each person

Chogyam Trungpa (1984) used the term "tender soft spot" to describe the core aspect of each person's human presence. Other names, carrying other nuances, include a person's *center, soul, basic goodness, inner self, or essence.* The basic idea is that this core human presence is knowable to both self and others via a felt sense.

The term "felt sense" was introduced by Gendlin (1978). In his psychotherapy research at the University of Chicago, Gendlin found that the best predictor of a therapy's session success, regardless of the therapy orientation, was whether the client experienced a "felt sense" in her body of the problem. This non-intellectual experience is not so much an emotional content as a bodymind feeling. As we will see, its presence is crucial to all aspects of self-relations therapy.

This notion of an original soft spot is an alternative to ideas like original sin, or to nothing at all. It can be experienced readily in an infant or a young child. Everybody has had the experience of being "turned on" by the presence of a young life. It can also be felt when a person is dying and her[1] defenses and masks have begun to dissolve. When this happens, an extraordinary feeling often fills the room and all its inhabitants. The experience is what

---

[1] The gender of singular pronouns is alternated by chapter throughout the book, with the feminine used in odd chapters and the masculine in even chapters.

Milton Erickson (1962/1980, p. 345) called "that vital sense of the beingness of the self (that) is often overlooked."

Jose Ortega y Gasset, the Spanish writer, was speaking to this sense in a conversation with a friend. They were talking about the woman Ortega y Gasset loved, and the friend asked him why he loved her. Ortega y Gasset replied that "I love this woman because she is *this* woman and no other. It is *this woman* that I love."

The idea of a center or tender soft spot is central to self-relations work. By definition, clients are caught in ways of thinking or acting that are painful and unsatisfying. In the problem area, their frames of reference aren't connecting with their strengths, resources, and confidences. Whatever they are doing to try to solve the problem is somehow making it worse. This suggests that they have lost connection to their center, to their own ways of knowing, to the place where they can feel renewed, resourceful, and confident.

That one's center is lost does not mean, however, that it is absent. To quote a phrase, you can check out any time you like, but you can never leave. In other words, your attention can move away from your center, but your center always remains right where it is.

One of the best pieces of evidence for the active presence of a center is the pain a person is experiencing. The experience of a symptom carries a core experience of pain in the body. This pain marks the spot and reveals the presence of the center. It may not have words; it may not have any acknowledgment at all, but it exists. We assume that such suffering is part of a "waking up" process: *life is always moving through the tender soft spot, helping the person to awaken more fully to her own goodness and to the goodness of the world.* Attempts to ignore or violate the tender soft spot create suffering. When the suffering is properly attended to, it will yield transformation and growth.

So the therapist begins by developing a felt sense of that center. As we will see, it's harder with some people than with others. Often, a client's story leads attention away from the center, so one has to be careful not to follow the words too literally. Feeling for tones and textures, the therapist receives the story to sense the place in the body from which the story is deflecting attention. As we will see, this is typically in the area of the heart, solar plexus, or belly.

As the therapist feels the client's center, she opens to its presence. It is like tuning into a drum beat or an energetic presence. This process includes finding and feeling the corresponding place inside the therapist. In other words, *the therapist's center is also felt and used to guide activities.* A main purpose of this connection is to stay connected with the person in a dynamic, moment-to-moment way. It is important to relax and open up to the person as well as to oneself, so different awarenesses, feelings, and conversations can move through the organic relational circuitry that has been established. This is akin to musicians playing together or to good friends talking. The notes or words change, but the underlying harmony and beat are sustained.

This centering process is calming for both therapist and client (cf. Richards, 1962). It allows a gentle focus and a connection to unconditional aspects of the person's presence, such as breathing and heartbeat.[2] It is especially helpful in releasing rigid holds on ideological positions, both the therapist's and the client's, thereby promoting a more flexible and honest relationship.

Intentionality can now be added. The self-relations therapist's intention is to join with the client to help her realize her goal(s). The therapist assumes that the client is "up to something big"; she is already moving in some important new direction, but it's being cut off in some way. When the therapist feels the nonverbal connectedness, her curiosity about where the client's going can translate into supporting each positive movement. The notion is that the client's inner self is already directing her in a positive way, but that her learned understandings have led her to reject, ignore, or attempt to negate this expression from her center. *This is the basis for the persistent suffering a client is experiencing.*

For example, one client was a man in his thirties. He was an outstanding musician and writer. He was smart, sensitive, with a great sense of humor. He had written hundreds of songs, many of

[2] The notion of an unconditional presence like breathing or heartbeat simply means that under all conditions of life, they are present. This is in contrast to any behaviors, thoughts, or feelings that are conditional, that is, they only occur under certain conditions. The suggestion here is that "the unconditional trumps the conditional," that is, if you can keep connectedness with the unconditional, the conditional will lose its negative charge.

them quite good. But every time he considered publishing or performing his songs in public, he was overwhelmed by what he called "receding into depression." This process included an intense pain in his belly, as well as negative self-criticisms that he was "resisting," "sandbagging," and "unwilling to face reality." Such processes are part of the texts that are used to dehumanize and otherwise violate the expressions from one's center. It led to his being "depressed" for months at a time. He hoped therapy would help him overcome his "resistance" and "childishness."

Assuming the pain was coming from his center, I followed some of paths described above to feel a connection with and curiosity about this center. The guiding idea was that his "depression" centered in his belly was actually part of the solution (not the whole solution, but a crucial element of it). A corollary idea was that he had learned, from experiences of violence or neglect, to reject the knowledge this "tender soft spot" provided him.[3] Now, more than ever, this other aspect of his self (what we will call the "neglected self") was insisting upon some direction. The practices of centering opened up a way to accept rather than fight it and to be curious about its contribution to his growth. As it turned out, the "receding self" in the belly was a call to go inside and reconnect in a different way before moving to the next step of actively presenting the self-revealing songs he had written.

So what we are saying here is that in addition to the cognitive self, the felt sense of a center in the somatic self is a place of knowing and responding effectively in the world. When a relationship to this center is lost, problems develop. When a person reconnects with the center, new experiences, understandings, and behaviors may emerge.

---

[3] *The Living Webster Encyclopedic Dictionary* defines "violence" as follows: "Intense or severe force; severe injurious treatment or action; an unfair exercise of power or force; an act of violence; an inordinate vehemence of expression or feeling; a distortion or misrepresentation of content, meaning, or intent." Relatedly, it defines "trauma" as: "from Gr. *trauma*, to wound; *Pathol.* a wound; a bodily injury produced by violence or some kind of shock; the condition produced by this; traumatism; *psychol.* a disordered or disturbed state, either mental or behavioral, which is an effect of some kind of stress or injury, and which sometimes has a lifetime effect." While the first definitions for each word occur commonly, the second are even more pervasive and epidemic. The idea here is that violence, whether physical or psychic, is a common relational event that casts a spell or curse upon a person that may last a long time. A major effect of this curse is the turning away from the tender soft spot, with devastating consequences. In this sense, every symptom reveals and replays an act of violence.

Premise 2: Life moves through you, except when it doesn't

> Once we see our place, our part of the world, as *surrounding* us, we have already made a profound division between it and ourselves. We have given up the understanding—dropped it out of our language and so out of our thought—that our land passes in and out of our bodies just as our bodies pass in and out of our land.
>
> —*Wendell Berry, 1977, p. 22*

A major reason for feeling the center is that it is through here that the river of life moves. The self extends into the world and the world enters into the self through the tender soft spot; it is a door between two realities. This ever-present psychic circulation is especially apparent in children. It seems like every experience known to humankind flows through a young child at least twice in each day! Every emotion is experienced, many different psychological frames are known, much is learned.

Similarly, artistic process emphasizes letting life move through you and guide you. An artist will talk about the importance of "just letting it happen." This is also the key idea in hypnotic work. Or in the martial art of aikido, where much practice is spent cultivating the capacity to feel "ki," or the "universal life force," flowing through you and connecting you with others. Similarly, a therapist may achieve a relaxed yet disciplined focus where thoughts, images, feelings, and sensations are circulating though, bringing suggestions, directions, resources, and other helpful hints and guesses.

This notion of life flowing through you has two aspects. One is a felt sense of an energetic presence or spirit that flows through everything. When felt, it provides harmony and connectedness. Musicians, athletes, and good friends know this feeling well. When dammed via muscular contraction and dissociation, one feels either depressed or increasingly overwhelmed by a seemingly foreign presence.

The second aspect is a psychological dynamic: every basic experience of being human will visit you, over and over again. There is nothing you can do to avoid it: simply by virtue of being alive, you will be touched repeatedly by sadness, happiness, anger, joy, disappointment, and so forth. Nobody escapes from such experiences, but each person (as well each culture, family, or relationship) develops particular ways to understand and relate to them. Some ways are helpful and allow growth; others are not helpful and result in what we will call ineffective suffering. Our challenge is to help people develop ways to accept, be with, and learn from each experience that life sends our way.

The idea of the river of life moving through us means that no single image can define us. The self is not a "wounded inner child," "a wise old woman," an unconscious supercomputer, or any other metaphor or "thing." Multiple descriptions are needed. Each is a poetic metaphor; none is a literal or exclusive form. When any metaphor is used literally or exclusively, problems tend to occur. We will return to this idea again and again.

When mind is felt as flowing through each of us, it is understood as connecting all of us. It is not a thing contained inside any of us. In the traditions of art, hypnosis, and meditation, a crucial process is to experience mental process as just happening, to find a way to accept and be with what is happening. In this view, mind is pulsating through you, suggesting a path of development both universal and particular. It provides all the requisite experiences, both pleasant and unpleasant, to become more fully human. Your mission, should you decide to accept it, is to learn how to read and cooperate with these mental "suggestions." Again, this view is similar to those described by artists. For example, the Israeli novelist Amos Oz (1995) noted:

> When I sit down to write a story I already have the people. What are called the "characters." Generally there is a man—or woman—at the centre, and others round about or opposite. I don't know yet what will happen to them, what they will do to each other, but they have converged on me and I am already involved in conversations, arguments, even quarrels with them. There are times when I say to them: get out of here. Leave me alone. You are not right for me and I am not right for you. It's too difficult for me. I'm not the right man. Go to somebody else.
>
> Sometimes I persist, time passes, they lose interest, perhaps they really do go to some other writer, and I write nothing.
>
> But sometimes they persist, like Michael's Hannah, for example: she nagged me for a long time, she wouldn't give up, she said,

look, I'm here, I shan't leave you alone, either you write what I tell you or you won't have any peace. (p. 185)

In a similar way, the life of the psyche (and its history of humankind) may be seen to flow through each person. As I sometimes joke with clients, life is out to get you. We might say that what it wants is for you to grow and develop into your full maturity and uniqueness. It provides experiences and relationships in a developmental sequence to allow this growth to occur. The challenge is to develop practices for welcoming, listening deeply, accepting, understanding, and expressing whatever life is giving us.

In this process, attending to the tender soft spot of the soul is helpful in a variety of ways. Centering can reconnect "mind," or what we will call the cognitive self—that is, the person's narratives, frames of references, decisions—with the "body," or what we will call the somatic self—that is, the felt sense of nature and archetypal presence. It helps the therapist feel the goodness implicit in whatever experience is happening for a person, and allows her to suggest to clients that they can feel and develop trust in a noncognitive place deep inside of them. It encourages an attitude of curiosity and acceptance rather than one of control and fear. Most of all, it reawakens the mystery of life, allowing a sense that we are not merely closed systems but open in relationship with presences greater than our egos. Each person's life, then, is an evolving tapestry woven out of organic threads that move through the center spot. As the therapist sits with a client, she wonders which new threads are emerging, and then looks to find ways to properly name and make room for them.

The caveat is that as life flows through you, it brings difficult or overwhelming experiences at times. So we have the capacity to shut down around the "tender soft spot," protecting it from damage. The problem, of course, is that shutting it down means that we are no longer connected to the pulse of life. Thus, a major goal of therapy is to help a person open herself to the world again, while learning skills of relatedness for how to deal with each experience that this connection with life brings.

Premise 3: Life is great, but sometimes it hurts like hell

The river of life brings both suffering and joy. Both are crucial to sense and be with in therapy. It is easy to get caught in one and ignore the other. For example, traditional therapy often focuses on the suffering and pain in a person and misses the strengths, resources, and happiness in a client's world. Solution-focused and other contemporary approaches are at risk of ignoring and rejecting the suffering of the person and the world. As Deng Ming-Dao (1992) reminds us:

> Sometimes what we learn is not pleasant. With learning, we glimpse life as it really is, and that is difficult to bear. That is why spiritual progress is slow: not because no one will tell us the secrets, but because we ourselves must overcome sentiment and fear before we can grasp it.
> There is an underbelly of terror to all life. It is suffering, it is hurt. Deep within all of us are intense fears that have left few of us whole. Life's terrors haunt us, attack us, leave ugly cuts. To buffer ourselves, we dwell on beauty, we collect things, we fall in love, we desperately try to make something lasting in our lives. We take beauty as the only worthwhile thing in this existence, but it cannot veil cursing, violence, randomness, and injustice. (p. 48)

When we are willing and able to be with each moment as it is—living life on life's terms—we sense that nothing is permanent, that change is already occurring. We develop a skill that the Buddhists call the agency of "mindfulness." It is a learned skill of enormous importance to psychotherapy. It requires a tender sobriety, a willingness to absorb each experience and then let it go. *Mindfulness is not so much a "doing" as the "being with" that precedes effective doing.* It is neither passive submission nor active resistance, but a learning how to live and love with a commitment to nonviolence. Once experiential understanding is developed, what the Buddhists call "right action" may emerge. This is a nonviolent expression from one's center that responds effectively to the various aspects of a given circumstance.

Since centering is a skill that no one ever perfects, many responses come from off-center. As the old Greek saying goes, we abandon our souls a hundred times, no, a thousand times each day. The problem occurs when we don't return to our center. For example, we may lose relatedness and "become" or identify with an experience. We see this in therapy in terms of being stuck in an emotional state or in some acting-out process. Or we might try to deny relatedness via dissociation, projection, denial, intellectualization, violence, and so forth. Here the person's presenting self (e.g., critical) is the opposite of her experiential process (e.g., fearful); that is, it is a compensation or denial of the primary (rejected) experience.

The problem is that an unintegrated response repeats itself until integrated. On this point, nature seems eternally patient and forever cruel. It may take years or even generations, but *a negative experience returns until human presence is brought to touch it with love and acceptance and integrate it.* When there is no mature human presence in relationship with it, it appears as an "out of control" process that must be gotten rid of. It assumes what Sam Keen (1986) has described as archetypal "faces of the enemy." In therapy, faces of the enemy include "depersonalized others" such as "anxiety" and "depression." Many therapists feel not only justified but obligated to obliterate any presences going by such impersonal names. Self-relations assumes that such a violent attitude toward the "other" is the basis for further suffering.

To identify this "neglected self," one can simply say: "*If only I could not do or experience X, then my life would work.*" "X" marks the spot of the unintegrated response. In self-relations, we inquire about this "neglected self," especially in terms of where it is felt in the body. This may not be immediately apparent or straightforward, since in self-protection the person has "spun off" from being in direct relationship with the suffering. In later chapters we will examine how to tune into and work with this neglected self.

Many fears and self-punitive processes are packed around the pain in the tender soft spot, so it is important to proceed with sensitivity. We will see how the therapist first connects with the client's center as well as her own as a basis for responding. Connecting to the noncognitive center is especially helpful for not getting caught in the narratives and judgments a client has about her experiences. It allows a therapist to sense where a client's suffering is centered, and then to open the corresponding place within herself. For example, if the client describes pain in the heart area, the therapist opens her own heart center and works to stay gently connected with it. This is both a self-protective and a therapeutic measure, for *each experience within the client opens up something in the therapist.* For example, if a client shares her sadness regarding the loss of a child, the therapist will likely feel some comparable sadness. This shared suffering is, of course, the basis of compassion, which self-relations holds as central to the therapeutic relationship. But while the therapist experiences suffering, she does not take on the self-negating narratives about the suffering.[4] This opens the possibility of shifting to a loving relationship with the experienced pain. In other words, rather than feeling fear or disappointment about the sadness, the therapist relates to it with love and curiosity. In this way, suffering is accepted as a major basis for increasing love for self and others. This in turn increases resilience, flexibility, and responsiveness to life's many challenges.

In dealing with suffering, it is equally important to keep in mind the joys, resources, and strengths of the person. Indeed, a major basis for the problem is that when suffering occurs the person forgets the rest of her life. Conversations that touch both the wounds/failures and the competencies/resources of a person create the experience of holding both at the same time. This initiates what Jung (1916/1971) called the transcendent function, which integrates opposites, and is another significant example of the relational self.

Suffering seems to be a very difficult idea to talk about. On the one hand, people may trivialize or disconnect from it, falsely believing that they can avoid it via some ideology or practice. On the other, it may be reified and regarded as part of one's life identity, used as a basis for self-flagellation or self-hatred. Neither extreme is helpful. Thomas Merton (1948) used to say that he did not become a monk to suffer *more* than other people, but

---

[4] The idea here is that a symptom includes (1) an experience of suffering, (2) cognitive frames or narratives about the meaning of the suffering, and (3) behavioral reactions (such as suppression and violent acting out) to the experience. These levels are usually undifferentiated in a symptom. The therapist works to differentiate them.

ather to suffer more effectively. Effective suffering means that you recognize and accept it as an unavoidable and helpful part of living in the world and growing as a person. It needn't be psychologized or regarded with pity or sentimentality; however, to deny its presence is extremely costly. So the challenge is how to touch it and name it and work with it effectively, without developing rigid ideological understandings or other compulsive control strategies.

The proof is in the pudding. In effective suffering, experience changes and self-love deepens as the heart cracks open to a deeper tenderness and centeredness. As the Buddhists say, the heart was meant to be broken, over and over again. Not shattered, but opened to a greater connection with self and world. In ineffective suffering, identity hardens and possibilities close. A good portion of the book is devoted to examining the role of effective suffering in psychotherapy.

Premise 4: There are two of you: Relationship is the basic psychological unit

Thus far, we have explicitly noted the presence of an indestructible "tender soft spot" at the core of each person. We have noted how life in all forms and all valences flows through this center. It is the basis for what we will call the archetypal mode of the somatic self, in that it draws upon the collective experiences of human being. For example, suppose a couple in therapy is struggling intensely with issues of intimacy. At one level, the struggle is unique to them. At another, the struggle is archetypal: it represents a struggle in the collective history of intimate relationships. No matter who the individuals are, the struggle for intimacy will occur. By accepting and understanding this archetypal level, one can also receive guidance and resources from the collective consciousness. We will see how connecting with the center of the somatic self allows some of these archetypal resources to emerge.

In addition to this archetypal (somatic) self, a second self develops over time in each person. This cognitive self, living more in the head and based more in social-cognitive-behavioral language, makes decisions, meanings, strategies, evaluations, and temporal sequences. It develops a description of one's competencies, preferences, and values. As we will see, the cognitive self typically predominates, except when self-identity is of primary concern—e.g., trauma, developmental transitions, art, or religious experiences. At such times, the deep feelings and archetypal processes of the somatic self emerge more powerfully. Therapy is a process for how to understand and work with the archetypal contributions of this somatic self.

If a person identifies only with the cognitive self, alienation from life as it "moves through the belly" will ensue, and fear and ineffective attempts to control will predominate. If the identification is with ongoing experience or with the somatic self, a person will be captured by emotion, trauma, and fantasy, suffering what the Jungians call "inflation of the archetype." *The relational self is the experience of both selves simultaneously, without an identification with either.* The relational self is non-local: it is not "in" the cognitive self or the somatic self. As Figure 1.1 shows, it is the field that holds and the spirit that connects different selves. Each person is a relationship between selves, rather than the position

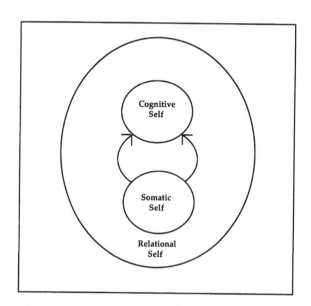

FIGURE 1.1. THE RELATIONAL SELF

of any given self. Also, the relational self is a shared field with other persons, so that the deeper unity with others may be sensed and realized in many ways.

The relational self has been noted in diverse contexts. Seymour Epstein (1994) reviewed a wide variety of research supporting a dual-processing or "double-mind" model of human being. William James used the "rider/horse" metaphor to describe it. Good parent/child or teacher/student relationships embody it. Art raises it to a beautiful level.

One way to understand how the connection between the somatic self and the cognitive self awakens the relational self may be found in the two German words for eating: "essen" and "fressen." Fressen is to "pig out," to eat like an animal; essen is to eat like a person. Using this distinction in a more general way, we might say that we begin with "fressen" energy (or "nature") and then bring human presence (or "mind") to transform it into "essen" (or human) expressions. The nature of fressen energy may be seen in a child's spontaneous joy, temper tantrums, expressive art, whining, innocent kindness, and innocent cruelty. It is apparent in the challenging psychological experiences of intense anger, irrational fear, inappropriate but compulsive behaviors, and psychological symptoms. It is also in the nature of storms, sunny days, animals, and flowers, and in wild celebrations, intense sexuality, and political rallies. Fressen energy is sometimes beautiful, sometimes horrible, sometimes both. Fressen energies carry the rhythms of time and change, as well as the archetypal forms of generational learnings.

Essen forms are the traditions, forms, and practices that have been developed within a culture, group, family, or person for receiving, molding, understanding, and expressing fressen energies. As we will see, an essen form may or may not be helpful for its users. Unhelpful forms will produce suffering and the need to evolve new essen forms.

We will also see how three relationships may be taken with "fressen energy": it may be stifled and oppressed, ignored and let run wild, or sponsored and cultivated into an artful expression. In aikido, these three response styles are called fight, flight, or flow. This third, middle way is the emphasis of self-relations. *It requires the agency of mindfulness and the skill of mature sponsorship.*

Fressen energy + sponsorship = artful human expressions

The principle of sponsorship is the most central skill of mature love, and so is a major emphasis of this book. (For example, Chapter 5 describes thirteen skills of sponsorship relevant to therapy.) We will emphasize two types of sponsorship: positive sponsorship and negative sponsorship. As Table 1.2 shows, positive sponsorship accomplishes three things. It awakens awareness of the self, awakens awareness of the world, and introduces skills and practices for forging a generative relationship between the two. As Table 1.3 shows, negative sponsorship has the opposite effect. Through neglect or violence, it (1) turns the person away from her own goodness, (2) convinces the person that the world is a terrible place that has no love or place for the person, and (3) introduces relational practices of denigration and violence. Except where explicitly noted, our discussion of sponsorship in therapy will regard the principles and practices of positive sponsorship. We will see how sponsorship, positive or negative, may be provided by self as well as many other people, institutions, and entities. We will see how in the absence of active positive sponsorship by self and others, negative sponsors will take over a person's life. Therapy is in no small part helping a person develop positive sponsorship of herself as well as the world in which she lives.

Sponsorship is different from ownership. It brings mindful human presence to fressen energy in a way that encourages and cultivates its expression without dominating or oppressing it. It acknowledges the "thou-ness" of the other while also maintaining relatedness. It is the challenge of the parent, the therapist, the artist, and the athlete. It is also the challenge of every individual trying to grow in personhood: how to accept and work with

---

TABLE 1.2. OUTCOMES OF POSITIVE SPONSORSHIP

1. Awakens awareness of self: its goodness, gifts, and longings
2. Awakens awareness of world: its goodness, gifts, and longings
3. Introduces skills and traditions to develop self-in-world and word-in-self: cultivating happiness and transforming suffering

---

TABLE 1.3. OUTCOMES OF NEGATIVE SPONSORSHIP

1. Ignores or violates self, deadening awareness of goodness.
2. Turns one away from the goodness and aliveness of the world
3. Introduces practices of abuse and neglect of self and world.

what is naturally given in ways that refine it without stifling it. Thus, every moment is an opportunity for sponsorship of life in self, others, and the world.

Early on in a person's life, sponsorship is largely assumed and modeled by those in charge: parents, teachers, community. If they ignore, reject, or violate a presence coming through one's center, it goes unnamed (and hence unknown) or else cursed as not fit for human society. (This presence may be an external other—a different gender, race, family, etc.—or an internal other, such as an emotion or way of being.) We become afraid of "it" (i.e., our awakening self), thinking its awakening will destroy us. This leads to a shutting down around the center, a dissociation from one's natural "fressen energy," and a spinning-off into some disconnected sense of self and world.

In other words, life moves through us, bringing us one form of fressen energy after another, but we can shut down our access and awareness to it and our acceptance of it. We can distort and attempt to negate these life energies moving through us. This defensive and hostile attitude usually evolves out of necessity, a result of earlier experiences too overwhelming to handle. In many ways a symptom represents a call to return to the center, this time with the skills and resources developed after the earlier exodus. In other words, while a person did not have the skills of sponsorship at earlier times, she generally does by the time therapeutic help is sought. As we will see in later chapters, self-relations assumes that in addition to a problem-defined self, each person also has a competency-based self. She may not realize it when the problem is present, so a major task in therapy is to access the competent and resourceful self of the client and invite it to "sponsor" and transform the unintegrated and unsponsored aspects of experience that are at the heart of the symptom. (Self is created in each moment that essen awareness and fressen energy—mind and nature—touch and harmonize.) This is why love is referred to as both a courage and a skill: it requires great commitment, tenderness, and discipline to use it under adversarial conditions (such as those in which the problems occur).

Some extraordinary examples of how sponsorship translates fressen energy into essen experience may be found in the autobiography of Helen Keller (1902/1988). After an illness at eighteen months left her blind and deaf, she had little or no connection with human experience. She described the next six years as a dark world of intense sensations, anger, self-absorption, and frustration. When she was seven, a sponsor came into her life:

> The most important day I remember in all my life is the one on which my teacher, Anne Mansfield Sullivan, came to me. I am filled with wonder when I consider the immeasurable contrasts between the two lives which it connects. . . .
>
> Have you ever been at sea in a dense fog, when it seemed as if a intangible white darkness shut you in, and the great ship, tense and anxious, groped her way toward the shore with plummet and sounding-line, and you waited with beating heart for something to happen? I was like that ship before my education began, only I was without compass or sounding-line, and had no way of knowing how near the harbour was. "Light! give me light!" was the wordless cry of my soul, and the light of love shone on me in that very hour. (p. 16)

With a remarkable skillfulness of love, Sullivan "sponsored" Keller, bringing human language to Keller's inner "fressen" experience. (In a not too dissimilar way, every child learns about her emotional experience through this relational process of naming. Kids do not know what they're feeling until they learn how to properly name feelings.) As Keller described it, *the world of human being began precisely at the point she realized language for her experience.* When she learned a sign for water, it literally created the experience of water in a new way.

> As the cool stream gushed over one hand she spelled into the other the word *water*, first slowly, then rapidly. I stood still, my whole attention fixed upon the motions of her fingers. Suddenly I felt a

misty consciousness of something forgotten—a thrill of returning thought; and somehow the mystery of language was revealed
to me. I knew then that "w-a-t-e-r" meant the wonderful cool
something that flowing over my hand. The living word awakened
my soul, gave it light, hope, joy, set it free! There were barriers
still, it is true, but barriers that could in time in time be swept
away.

. . . I recall many incidents of the summer of 1887 that followed my soul's sudden awakening. I did nothing but explore with
my hands and learn the name of every object that I touched; and
the more I handled things and learned their names and uses, the
more joyous and confident grew my sense of kinship with the rest
of the world. (pp. 18–19)

In the same way, self-relations assumes that *an experience or
expression will not be seen to have human value until a loving
and mature human presence touches it and properly names it.*
The skill of sponsorship is thus crucial to working in therapy
with experiences and behaviors that apparently have no human
value (i.e., symptoms). As we will see, sponsorship involves seeing them, touching them, providing place and name for them,
connecting them with resources, connecting them with traditions
of expression, and other forms of skillful love.

We should be clear that in effective sponsorship fressen energy
is not denied or overcome. It is "included and transcended," as
Ken Wilber (1995) puts it. That is, it is still there, but something
else—human presence and rational love—is added. It is this relationship that awakens its human value and its potential for graceful expression. When this relationship is not present, the experience or behavior will be seen to have no human value. This is
where the therapy begins—with being aware of the persistent
"fressen energy" (i.e., the symptom) that needs sponsorship. As
we will see, the skills of sponsorship then promote the integration
and transformation of this "fressen energy" into positive "essen
expressions."

Many examples of how this might be done are given in this
book. For now we may say that, when the therapist sits with a
person, a felt connection to the center is developed. The therapist
then listens to what the person's narratives are saying about it.
Usually, the experience in one's center is being devalued or ne-

glected in some way, so the therapist begins gently to challenge that. She asks where a person learned to think or talk that way about the experience in question, and whether it has been helpful or not. Many times people say it hasn't been helpful, but it beats the alternative of being overwhelmed by it. So a relationship distinguished by violence and subjugation begins to emerge, wherein the "other" is seen as an "it" that needs to be destroyed. The self-relations therapist is interested in how this violence and the consequent suffering may be alleviated by sponsoring each of these different "its" so they may be translated into "thous." This is akin to couples therapy, where the differences between positions are seen as essential to creative growth. The key is validating and giving respect to each position, challenging and transforming violent expressions toward the other, and grounding the description in bodymind rhythms and feelings.

An important assumption in this work is that the somatic self—the source of fressen energy—isn't an extension or part of the cognitive self. It is a part of the larger relational self, but has its own autonomous life, in many ways different from the cognitive self. Again, the comparison to a mate is helpful. For example, it matters whether I regard Denise, my wife, as "Denise" first and "my wife" second, or the other way around. Similarly, when we regard the "other self" as autonomous, we can begin to realize that life moves through him or her. Our mission thus is to feel the center in our body that embodies this self and to listen and sense the life flowing through it, responding to it without identification or dissociation. Our soul is "waking up" to a deeper awareness, and the task of the cognitive self is to "be with" and sponsor this awakening of life.

This is a central idea for therapy. It leads to an appreciation that the gift of life is given anew in each and every breath. It may be cursed and attacked, but the symptom as well as the resources wonderfully reveal that such violent attempts at suppression ultimately fail. The gift of life lives on! This realization allows one to surrender to a deeper presence, to be grounded and connected with an inner center that, when felt and cultivated, provides a more vital and effective sense of self. The legacy of violence into which the person was recruited can now be replaced with traditions and practices of self-love.

Premise 5: An intelligence greater than you exists in the world

> The individual mind is immanent but not only in the body. It is immanent also in pathways and messages outside the body; and there is a larger Mind of which the individual mind is only a subsystem. This larger Mind is comparable to God and is perhaps what some people mean by "God," but it is still immanent in the total interconnected social system and planetary ecology.
>
> —*Gregory Bateson, 1972, p. 461*

> The purpose of the journey is compassion. When you have come past the pairs of opposites, you have reached compassion.
>
> —*Joseph Campbell, in Osbon, 1991, p. 24*

We have thus been talking about two sources of intelligence that a person draws from: (1) the awakening inner center (and fressen energies) of the somatic self and (2) the sponsorship (and essen forms) of the cognitive self. Yet a third source beyond the relational self is equally important. Simply stated, self-relations assumes that there exists a power and presence greater than the intellect or individual in the world.

This topic is, astonishingly enough, the basis for the greatest contributions as well as the greatest violence ever committed. So we must be very careful in how we address it. But address it we must, for the consequences of not doing so are equally disastrous. The simple idea is that in isolation a person is not enough. By yourself, you are incompetent, inadequate, and impotent. As the existentialists say, psychopathology is precisely the study of loneliness. When a person has a sustained break in relatedness to something bigger than herself, problems will occur. Conversely, a reconnection to a relational field that supports and nurtures a person is crucial for therapeutic change.

While this relational field is universal, it has no fixed form. Each person comes to know this field in her own way, and these ways change over time. Thus, *the relational field must always be understood in therapy in the way the client understands it.* Its value is in its vitality: as soon as it becomes part of a dogma, ideology, or system, this value is lost and replaced by deadening understandings. Thus, therapy must always strive to develop a felt sense of the field, regarding all descriptions of it as poetic terms whose value is in their capacity to touch a living presence of life.

A client may know the field through the experience of children, and hence call it innocence. She may have found it through political kinship, and thus call it justice. He may know it through the experience of trance, and call it the unconscious. She may know it through athletic mastery, and call it "the zone." He may know it through marriage or friendship, and call it love. She may know it through religious practice, and call it God. She may know it through walking on the beach or in the mountains, and call it nature.

The important thing is that virtually all humans know an experience of a power and presence greater than themselves. Self-relations simply makes the observation that problems disappear in these experiences (of prayer, community, trance, dancing, breathing, walking, touching, etc.). We examine what happens during those states that allow well-being and the dissolution of a problem-defined self. We notice that in these states, a person invariably feels an expanded sense of self and that, paradoxically, a greater sense of confidence develops even as boundaries soften.

We then wonder if and how this relational field may be developed when the "problem" is being experienced. In later chapters we will examine techniques for bringing the problem into the relational field in order to transform the problem. We ask clients about their felt sense of this relationship field and note how they describe a feeling of well-being that surrounds them. We suggest it may be helpful to think of this felt field as a living, nurturing presence that supports a person in her awakening process. In other words, *the field is alive and wants to help you become more of your self.* You are responsible for your choices and behaviors, but this "higher power" (as you understand it) is there to help. We explore what it would be like to trust and tune into an intelligence greater than the isolated intellect. We identify how a person is already doing that in other areas of her life, and how those practices and understandings may be used in the problem area. We emphasize carefully the differences between regressive collapses and mature surrender to (and active participation in) something greater than one's own ego. In this regard, we emphasize the equal importance of a center and a cognitive self.

Therapists must be especially sensitive with language in this area, for any literalization will be counterproductive. A field is not a "thing" and thus cannot be concretized. Any term used— love, God, nature, community, field—is a poem pointing to an experience that is ineffable but quite real to most people. As we will see throughout the book, attention to this relational field can be extremely helpful in the therapeutic process.

Premise 6: Your path is yours alone: You are an incurable deviant

One of the concerns many clients have is that they are, at least in the areas of their problems, weird and strange. I try to find ways to assure people (with a sympathetic Irish twinkle) that they have understated the matter tremendously. They're a lot weirder than their deepest fears suggest and it's only going to get worse! Again, this is said in a loving way and only when it seems that a client can sense the intent of validating her unique ways of knowing and being.

One of the obvious implications is that a person will have to face the fact that she cannot meet other people's expectations. This signals the end of what might be called the "camel" phase of human development. I believe it was Nietschze who suggested that for the first part of life, we are camels, trudging through the desert, accepting on our backs everybody's "shoulds" and "don'ts." Camels only know how to spit; they don't think for themselves or talk back. As the camel dies, a lion is born in its place. Lions discover both their roar and the art of preening. The lion may be a little shaky at first, so support and encouragement are vital. But once the camel begins to die (e.g., signaled by depression), there is no turning back. Symptoms occupy the space between the death of the camel and the birth of the lion. A therapist can be a good midwife during this liminal phase.

Joseph Campbell used to say that sometimes you climb the ladder to the top, only to discover that you've placed it against the wrong wall. A symptom is such a message. It says that the way a person has viewed or expressed life no longer fits. Something or somebody inside is urging the person to find a new way. The "essen forms" of knowing and doing are being overwhelmed by the life-giving "fressen energies." To effectively receive and be transformed by these new energies, one must first climb down off the ladder set against the wall of other people's expectations. Few if any of us do this willingly; a symptom forces us to do so.

One of the benefits of accepting your "deviancy" (or uniqueness) is that you can ease the endless self-demands for change. Wanting to change can be a form of self-hatred, stemming from the hope that "If only I were different from who I am now, then you would love me." Endless attempts to perform in hopes of love result in the horrible realization that you have failed. If you can open your heart to the pain of life, you will realize that it's not about you; it's the nature of the beast. Symptoms such as depression are remarkable voices of integrity at this time. They signal that "nothing will work," "it doesn't matter," and "there's no use." This signals the death of an illusory self that, if properly accepted and dealt with, can lead to reconciliation between the cognitive self and the somatic self. A need for a solid container is crucial at this point, for the dangers of acting out in violence are substantial. But the cry of a symptom is an expression in part of the need to accept some unique, unacknowledged aspect(s) of oneself.

I sometimes suggest to clients that hypnosis teaches you just how wonderfully and incurably weird you really are. In hypnosis, each person does it her own way. The therapist suggests one thing, but when things are working properly, the client responds with something else. Therapy really begins when the client is not following the therapist's way, but discovering her own way. In a larger sense, life really begins when one is defeated by a presence greater than the ego. As Rilke (1981b) lamented:

> What we choose to fight is so tiny!
> What fights with us is so great!
> If only we would let ourselves be dominated
> as things do by some immense storm
> we would become strong too, and not need names. (p. 105)

Without resistance or failure, therapy (and life) is usually a polite social game. Failure and wounding open us to a deeper presence within ourselves and in the world, to a greater wisdom and intelligence.

Therapy is a conversation about how to sense this deeper wisdom. It assumes that each person has her own path, her own unique way, and that the symptoms are part of that path of self-development. Since the therapist's way of knowing and experiencing is different, the success of therapy is predicated on the failure of the therapeutic theory and technique. The therapist is at best a sort of "holy fool" who knows that while her way is not the client's way, she must proceed with dignity nonetheless, waiting for the client to "push back" the theory and technique in order to reveal a different perspective, one that is more true for the client.[5] The capacity to accept and hold these differences leads to good therapy. It also leads to an increasing appreciation that each client must discover her own uniquely deviant way of knowing and being in the world.

Summary

The six premises described above may be very helpful in the process of doing therapy. They stem from an appreciation of what Trungpa (1984) has called the indestructible "original soft spot" (as compared to "original sin") that is the core of each human being. When the soft spot is violated or neglected, pain occurs. To avoid being overwhelmed by pain, a person spins off a persona (including a story line) that lives some distance from one's center. For many of us, our sense of identity has been founded on the denial of the original soft spot. The mental agitation and distortion arising from this denial produce suffering, which generates further agitation and distortion, and away we go, sometimes only returning years or even generations later.

This dissociation from one's center is initially a solution. Not

---

[5] A good example of a "holy fool" was Gandhi, who went to see the King of England dressed only in a loin cloth. When asked about this, he dryly noted that he thought the King was wearing enough clothes for the both of them. Later, when asked what he thought of Western civilization, Gandhi replied, "I think it would be an excellent idea!"

only does it numb the pain of the somatic self, but it also leads to the development of a separate cognitive self. As the person develops resources, however, the continued alienation from the somatic self (and the world) becomes a liability, for a better way is now available. This better way involves a relational self that connects the sponsorship capacities of the cognitive self with the life-giving "fressen energies" of the somatic self. This is what a symptom attempts to do for a person: it is a "call to return" to the original center and an opportunity to move into an integrated, relational self. What it requires is a surrender of the power principle, a willingness to engage and sponsor the other (interior or exterior) self without violence. Unfortunately, a person generally has been led to believe that surrender (or "letting go") would be a disaster, so she continues to resist the river of fressen energies moving through her being. On this point nature seems eternally patient: she simply waits, and then begins the healing cycle again. At some point, a person feels that control is slipping away and comes to a therapist in desperation.

Clients thus come to therapy already engaged in the process of change. *Some important identity change is already in motion that they cannot stop.* Or as we say in self-relations, the person is "up to something big." Something is waking up inside the person. The problem is that the person has been conditioned to neglect or violate herself in this process, thereby temporarily stopping the awakening process. She has learned to distrust or ignore herself and the relational field that holds her. Sponsorship of a solution involves a paradoxical relationship of "not resisting" (allowing experience to flow through) while "not becoming" (not identifying with the experience). The relational self is a field that holds two selves, one to be mindful of what is and the other to "experience" the river of life moving through. From this relational self, a middle way between repression and acting out is cultivated, and life is no longer a problem (for a while).

Entering a session with these premises, the therapist drops attention into her center and then opens attention to be with the client with curiosity about where the unsponsored but dominant "fressen energy" is. From this centered place, both suffering and resources may be felt, held, named, and otherwise sponsored. To do this, the therapist keeps in mind that the client is a relationship between different selves. Therapy then explores how a spirit of connectedness between these selves may be felt and fostered. Neuromuscular locking—a freezing of the mindbody—will prohibit this spirit of connection, so methods for relaxing the lock are used. As this happens, the therapist joins, blesses, and works with whatever is happening, knowing the solution is already in motion.

2

ATTENTION AND THE RELATIONSHIP

BETWEEN DIFFERENCES

HOW DO WE DEAL WITH THE OTHER?

> One day a man approached Ikkyu and asked: "Master, will you please write for me some maxims of the highest wisdom?"
>
> Ikkyu took his brush and wrote, "Attention."
>
> "Is that all?" asked the man.
>
> Ikkyu then wrote: "Attention. Attention."
>
> "Well," said the man, "I really don't see much depth in what you have written."
>
> Then Ikkyu wrote the same word three times: "Attention. Attention. Attention."
>
> Half-angered, the man demanded: "What does that word "Attention" mean, anyway?"
>
> Ikkyu gently responded, "Attention means attention."
>
> *—In Schiller, 1994*

ON OUR JOURNEY through this world, we are constantly faced with differences—different truths, different needs, different forms of expressions, different paths. In therapy, these differences might be the way things are and the way I want them to be; for example, a couple wants a child and yet cannot conceive. It could be a difference between my truth and your truth; for example, the same couple may look at their marriage in two seemingly contradictory ways. It might be a difference between what others say—

you're this way or that way—versus what a person intuitively feels about himself. Or it may be between what the therapist feels is the "problem" or the correct solution and what the client feels to be the case.

How we attend to such differences is a primary basis for self-identity. We may use violence or nonviolence in our relational approach, with the consequences of deepening suffering or gradual developmental growth. In this view, relationship is the basic psychological unit of discourse. As Jung (1969) noted:

> The unrelated human being lacks wholeness, for he can achieve wholeness only through the soul, and the soul cannot exist without the other side, which is always found in a "You." Wholeness is a combination of I and You, and these show themselves to be parts of a transcendent unity whose nature can only be grasped symbolically, as in the symbol of the *rotundum*, the rose, the wheel, or the *conjunctio Solis et Lunae* (the mystic marriage of sun and moon). (p. 39)

Figure 2.1 offers a simple illustration of this basic unit. The two small interconnected ovals within a larger field suggest at least four perspectives on any given experience: (1) the values, experiences, truths, positions, etc., held in the first circle ("self" or "me"); (2) the values, experiences, truths, positions, etc., held in the second circle ("otherself" or "not-me"); (3) the relation-

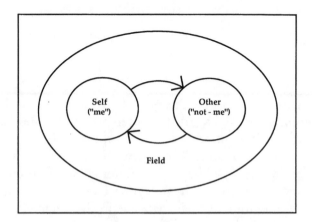

FIGURE 2.1. THE BASIC UNIT OF PSYCHOLOGICAL DISCOURSE

ship between the two positions; and (4) the field in which they are held.

Besides indicating different aspects of any relational experience, these perspectives represent a progression of four psychological awarenesses in each learning cycle: the felt existence of an "I"; the felt existence of a "thou"; the felt existence of an interconnectedness between the different beings; and the felt existence of a deeper presence supporting the differences. Each of these perspectives carries a different way of understanding, a different meaning, a different value. By progressing through each perspective, a person may develop an ecological knowing that leads to greater integrity, responsiveness, and happiness. A learning cycle may be completed, new learnings integrated, and the field cleared to allow the wheel of learning to begin again, with a new set of differences, conflicts, and learnings emerging.

For example, the question might be raised as to what's more important, being independent or being interdependent. It's a trick question, for each completes the other. (A general principle in self-relations is that everything contains its opposite.) One without the other is pathological: agency by itself leads to dominance, isolation, and loneliness; communion by itself leads to submission, isolation, and loneliness. Being separate leads to the need to be in communion, and vice versa. If a relational "conversation" between these needs is allowed to develop over time, a deeper unitive experience of "agency-in-communion" is likely to emerge (Wilber, 1995). This "making of love" between complementary truths gives birth to a new experience of self, one that "transcends yet includes" each of its members (Wilber, 1995).[1] A new cycle of learning begins, with a new set of differences.

Obviously, all is not smooth in this developmental journey. We may become overwhelmed, distracted, misguided, inattentive, or otherwise out of sorts. Violence or fear may arrest movement at any place in the progression, leading to contraction, suffering,

---

[1] Wilber (1995) uses the term "transcends and includes" in his developmental model of consciousness, borrowing Koestler's (1964) term of "holon" to describe a concentric developmental progression where each distinction is both a "part" and a "whole." That is, each distinction contains other distinctions and is in relation to other distinctions at the same level (and thus has autonomy and agency), while at the same time being a part of a distinction at a higher level (and thus has the property of communion). In this view, everything is connected to everything, though there are different levels of distinction. One can ascend up through levels or descend down through levels.

and unwitting repetition of the undesired state. A person may become attached to a particular perspective, against all others. Violence against self and/or others is often used, deliberately or unwittingly, to maintain this stuck state.

Therapists come into people's lives at exactly such points. The violence we see may take many forms—the self-abuses of addiction, dissociation, self-hatred, depression, or the abuse of others. The hope in using violence is that we can eliminate the "other" and thereby create peace. But violence does not eliminate anything; it strengthens the presence of the other and distorts its nature. No long-term solution is found, and another cycle of damaging conflict begins. Our mission is to bring mindfulness and sponsorship to these places of violence, so that more effective and less painful responses may develop.

Many skills and perspectives are available for doing this. This chapter focuses on how different ways of attending to relationship may harm or help development. We will be guided by the Errol Flynn principle, named after the swashbuckling actor of movie fame. When asked about the correct way to hold a sword, Flynn replied that one should imagine holding a bird instead of a sword. If you hold too tight, he said, the bird dies and the life is lost; if you hold too loose, the bird escapes and flies away and you're left with nothing.

As with birds and swords, so with life. We will see how holding attention "too tight" results in viewing differences as irreconcilable and leads to the violence of fundamentalism. Then we will look at how holding "too loose" encourages indifference to others and may lead to the despair and emptiness of consumerism as a lifestyle. Finally, we will see how holding attention "not too tight, not too loose" may allow the generative spirit of love to emerge and solutions and reconciliations to develop.

Holding too tight: The fear and fury of fundamentalism

> In my solitude
> I have seen things very clearly
> That were not true
>
> —*Antonio Machado, 1983*

The first perspective in a learning cycle is identification with a particular perspective or "truth." We find something that brings a feeling of aliveness, excitement, hope, or possibility. It could be the scientific method or the religious teachings of the Bible. It could be the work of Milton Erickson or the music of the Grateful Dead. It might be our ethnic tradition, our gender knowledge, or our national history. It could be the principle of power or the principle of cooperation, the idea of materialism or that of spirituality. Whatever the content, we begin to identify ourselves with this position, this path, this truth.

This identification with a perspective provides a ground to stand on, a frame to see from, and a knowledge to speak from. It gives a unique perspective on the world and offers hope that, if we stick with it, good things will happen. It allows us to make progress in our skillfulness and suggests a coherent way of knowing and being. But if rigidified into an ideology, it gives rise to competition, specialization, isolation, contraction, and fixation. If held too long or too tightly, these values will create significant problems.

Such problems arise when life brings us values and experiences different from those with which we are identified. (And in contemporary life, this is evermore the rule, not the exception.) We may feel that if we leave our little circle of identification and open to another way of knowing or being, bad things—chaos, loss of self, overwhelming fear, death—will follow. This fear may deepen our conviction that only our way is right and all others are wrong. If held rigidly, this belief will progress into seeing violence as the only possible relationship between different ways.

Perhaps the clearest version of this approach to relational differences is fundamentalism. Fundamentalism emphasizes orthodoxy (from "ortho," right, and "dox," belief) as primary.[2] What's inside of one little circle (in Figure 2.1) is the right belief and what's outside of it is dangerous and wrong. The consciousness

---

[2] Fundamentalism first arose as a conservative Protestant movement in early twentieth-century America. Its adherents were shaken by the growing relativism of modernist society and insisted that there were certain unchangeable "fundamentals" that must be rigidly observed and defended. There are now many different fundamentalist movements in virtually every religious school. We are using the term a bit more generally here, to describe any psychological approach that vehemently insists upon an unchanging text as the one and only "objective truth" (see Strozier, 1994).

of the observer (and the observed) is irrelevant or, at best, subordinate to the correct belief. The river of fressen energy, or anything natural, is oppressed, controlled, feared, and violated, since this river is forever changing the nature of experience and understanding. The ideology of "truth" or what "should be," rather than the experience of consciousness or relationship, is the operative metaphor. As a general (and perhaps the most common) approach to experience, *the ideology of fundamentalism is not limited to any specific content or beliefs.* It is not specifically a "right-wing" or "religious" approach. It can be applied to any set of content, any theory or description, including those explicitly positing non-fundamentalist tenets (such as the present one). There are undoubtedly as many "liberal" fundamentalisms as "conservative" ones, as many secular as religious ones, and so forth. Indeed, fundamentalism is used by each of us many times each day, each time we close our hearts and minds to the present moment and to different truths. Because it is such a clear example of the ideologies that form from holding too tight, it is worth a closer examination.

Fundamentalism starts with the premise that identity is defined according to allegiance to some single truth. This truth is revealed in a special text. I use the term "text" loosely here, meaning any frame of words, images, and feelings. The therapist's theory is a text; so is each memory, experience, or story of the client. In fundamentalism, a particular text is assumed to reveal THE truth, rather than a truth. Identity is based on strict adherence to that truth. The text is more important than experience itself, so in fundamentalism the primary relationship of a person is with the unchanging single text, rather than with the organic here and now of life itself. Needless to say, this makes learning difficult, if not impossible.

Fundamentalism further requires that the text be read literally: it is not to be sensed poetically, metaphorically, or with a sense of humor.[3] (You never hear about a funny fundamentalist comic or a

---

[3] An especially relevant example of this concerns psychotherapy theories. There are well over a hundred distinct psychotherapy approaches, each asserting its own version of truth. I suggest it would be a lot more helpful to regard each theory as a poem rather than a scientific fact. We would not consider arguing over which is the right poem, but would be more interested in how a given poem touched and opened the experience of a particular listener.

poignant fundamentalist artist.) In fundamentalism, psychological identity is expressed by fixating on the text, rather than seeing or feeling through it to a deeper, aesthetic meaning. Thus, the metaphor of a inner child, the idea of an unconscious mind, a depression, or a solution is taken literally, rather than as a poem or metaphor that points beyond itself to something more ineffable, something more primary. In the words of William Blake (in Yeats, 1905/1979), "Satan has many names, Opacity being the most common."

In positing that one way is correct and all others are wrong, fundamentalism sees the relationship between differences as irreconcilable opposites. You are either an insider or an outsider in relation to the Truth; the possibility of relatedness across the boundaries is forbidden. If intimacy involves the holding of two different "truths"—the I and the thou, self and other—in relationship, then intimacy is disallowed. If creative activity— whether it be humor, art, or scientific discovery—involves the holding of two different frames simultaneously, then creative activity and aesthetic experience are forbidden.[4] If altered states of consciousness such as hypnosis are developed by assuming that a person has two different selves, then trance is to be feared.

The idea that differences are irreconcilable spells trouble when differences touch each other, as they have a habit of doing. (As Bateson emphasized, difference is the basic unit of mental process.) In fact, the I-it relationship given to my position and your different position is one of the better formulas for violence. The position of the "other" is deemed invalid in a way that legitimizes attempts to eliminate it by any means necessary.

An important aspect of this invalidation of the other is a belief in its irreversible or unchangeable nature. As Thomas Merton (1964) noted, oppression—whether it be of self or others—is founded upon the premise in the "irreversibility of evil"; that is,

---

[4] This idea of holding double frames simultaneously as the basis for the distinctly human experiences of humor, love, mythology, intimacy, craziness, play, etc., has been suggested by a variety of writers. Bateson's (1979) idea of "double description" as a minimal requirement for an ecological view, stemming from his earlier work on the double bind hypothesis, was central to his later work. Jung (1916/1971) suggested the idea of the transcendent function, involving the capacity to hold opposite truths simultaneously, as the basic means of individuation. And Arthur Koestler (1964), in his opus *The Act of Creation*, suggested the idea of bissociation, involving the holding and integrating of two disparate matrices, as the essential mechanism of creative activity.

once something is bad, sick, crazy, wrong, it will always be that way. If we accept that, then we are morally obliged to eliminate it. The thinking is: there's only room in this here self for one of us, so it might as well be you (rather than me) that is destroyed. In fact, destroying you will give me new life and greater freedom. This gives rise to a series of "final solutions" that seek, in the name of freedom, purity, mental health, justice, or God, to eradicate the bad, sick, crazy, or evil Other. Our image of the other is degraded into the archetypal face of the enemy (see Keen, 1986). Once the image of the enemy is locked into neuromuscular freeze, any "freedom-loving" person will feel not only justified but obligated to engage in violence to eradicate it.

In the clinical context, a client struggling with a symptom is a person struggling with, among other things, fundamentalism. For example, say a person has experienced a sexual trauma. In an almost unavoidable way, the memories or images of the trauma become imprinted as the text (or frame) by which future sexual or intimate relationships are understood. The traumatic memory becomes the fundamentalist text, which says that all relationships are like this, you can't trust anybody. Furthermore, the text of the memory is regarded as an "it" that a person may try to keep out of himself, though it keeps coming back (via flashbacks, repeated trauma, similar relationships, etc.).

The therapist's response to the client may be equally fundamentalist. The therapist may match the client's reports to a *DSM* checklist and represent the relationship as "treatment of a PTSD case," rather than as working with a unique person who has certain goals. Therapy may be strictly by the book, rather than through intimate conversations with a human being.

As therapists, we need to have compassionate understanding of how fundamentalism develops. *The "break in relatedness" between self and other occurs via violence or neglect and requires violence (against self and/or others) or neglect to continue.* We need to appreciate how the consequent reduction of identity to an image or an "ism" is a recipe for suffering and violence, and commit ourselves to exploring how the chain of violence may end and suffering relieved.

Self-relations is grounded in the realization that violence, no matter how justified it seems to be, is the surest way to create more violence. We are thus primarily interested in nonviolence as a guiding principle of action. When people think of nonviolence, they often conjure up images of ineffectual passivity or syrupy sentimentality. But the force of nonviolence, what Ghandi called *satyagraha* (meaning force or firmness of soul or heart or truth), is a quite vibrant and active presence. To differentiate it from weakness, we will first examine how relational problems may also compound by being too loose or too soft.

Holding too loose: The indifference and addiction of consumerism

While there is danger in holding relational experience too tightly, there is equal danger in not holding tight enough. Having too loose a connection to life may manifest in many ways. You may not be able to feel, or be willing to hold, the tension of opposites. The "thouness" of the other is forgotten, leading to an indifference to life and its delicate balances. Clarity of vision is lost, as feelings and thoughts drift by like tumbleweed in a mean-ingless wasteland. To quote Yeats, "the center cannot hold/ things fall apart/ mere anarchy is loosed upon the world."

Of the many lifestyle or ideological forms this looseness and indifference may take, the psychology of consumerism (and its attendant practice of advertising) is the most dominant. In con-sumerism, the "significant other" is an "it" to be acquired (e.g., money) or "an-other" to be devoured and used for one's enter-tainment, as in "I want another car, house, beer, potato chip, wife, trophy, toy, therapy theory, etc." The idea is that the indi-vidual ("me") is the basic unit, not relationship or community. In consumerism, fulfillment and satisfaction are claimed to be the result of acquiring more "things." If I get that job, I'll be happy. If I consume that drug, I'll be happy. If I buy those clothes, I'll feel better. If I read more books, I'll feel smarter. When consump-tion doesn't produce well-being, advertising promises that it is just a matter of consuming more. (As Bob Dylan used to say, money doesn't talk, it swears.) Privacy (from the Latin "depri-vare," or "to deprive the community of") is prized: privacy (and isolation) of thought, property, and feeling. Communitas—sharing with others, participating in community—and the realities of interconnectedness and interbeing are devalued. The downward spiral of addiction is spun, culminating in depression, exhaustion, and cynical indifference to life. (Long live Howard Hughes.)

A major component of consumerism is the idea of "maxima, not optima." More is better: more choices, more TV channels, more money, more information, more therapy, more power. More shoes, more words, more food, more drugs. More pity, more enemies, more rage, more acting-out. Questions like, "How would you know you've had enough?" "When would you be satisfied?" go unanswered as the pace of consumerism accelerates. Relationship is focused on consuming "an other," and human values and connections suffer. Materialism (from "mater" or mother) translates relationship into "I want/I deserve/I need to have all my needs satisfied." Naturally, this leads to an inattentiveness to life outside one's own immediate interest, and isolation and loneliness result. In therapy, consumerism places the question, "What do you want?" above all others. The question, "What does life want from you?" is ignored altogether.

A closely related value to "more is better" is "faster is better." Faster cars, briefer therapy, fast foods, instant enlightenment, quick fixes, rapid deterioration. Computer time replaces body time, and everything spins more rapidly, going nowhere but into greater confusion and depression.

In consumerism, the key relational dynamic of "giving and receiving" is perverted into selling and buying. A person works all day, if he can—selling himself to entities that use his labor to produce goods—and then comes "home" to "relax" by consuming mass quantities of "goods." Art is replaced by advertising, poetry by jingles, debate by posturing, love by sentimentality and indulgence, sexuality by pornography, struggle by convenience, humor by sarcasm and mocking, and participation by spectatorship. In short, citizens become consumers, focused on the pursuit of happiness through material consumption and acquisition.

There is, of course, nothing inherently wrong with material comfort and convenience. Indeed, material pleasures, sensuality, and comfort are integral parts of a life worth living. But ironically, consumerism actually turns one away from the material world. It encourages us to exploit and be indifferent toward the actual materials of the earth. Material goods are increasingly not appreciated for their workmanship, but mass produced, consumed, and discarded.

When consumerism is adopted as an ideology and dominant lifestyle, its pathologies and shortcomings are impressive. From a relational point of view, consumerism tends to isolate people into the self-absorption of pursuing gratification of desires. The most "significant other" is often a product to be consumed, rather than a person to be listened to and connected with. Equally damaging, one's own self is seen as a commodity to be exploited, rather than a gift of life to be nurtured and enjoyed. Discipline, tenderness, commitment, patience, listening, humility, and non-action are not valued in the fast-paced consumer world.

A major casualty of consumerism is language, especially imagery. A key aspect of consumerism is the fixation on, and exploitation of, the image. Baudrillard (1995) cogently described how imagery has evolved (or devolved) through four stages: (1) it first reflects a basic reality, (2) then it masks and perverts a basic reality, (3) then it masks the absence of a basic reality, and finally (4) it bears no relation to any reality whatsoever. In this last stage, discourse is not about truth and reality; it is the manipulation of symbols to stimulate. In short, images become an addictive drug. Talk shows and political speeches are obvious examples of this; psychotherapy is always a candidate.

When we can't see through the image to a deeper meaning of life, as in poetry or art, cynicism, mockery, and more materialism result.[5] As Bateson (1972) warned:

> Mere purposive rationality unaided by such phenomena as art, religion, dream, and the like, is necessarily pathogenic and destructive of life; and . . . its virulence springs specifically from the circumstance that life depends upon interlocking *circuits* of contingency, while consciousness can see only such short arcs of such circuits as human purpose may direct. . . .

[5] A major tenet of postmodernism is that there is no deeper meaning, or at the very least, no deep structure. Two of the major quotes in postmodernism are Wittgenstein's (1951, p. 89) "That whereof we cannot speak, we must remain silent," and Derrida's (1977, p. 155) "There is nothing outside the text." Rather than encouraging silence and a curiosity about the "nothingness," these quotes are often taken as discouraging the delicate task of discerning sub- or con-textual meaning.

> Unaided consciousness must always tend toward hate; not only because it is good common sense to exterminate the other fellow, but for the more profound reason that, seeing only arcs of circuits, the individual is continually surprised and necessarily angered when his hard-headed policies return to plague the inventor. (p. 146)

In consumerism, language is further divorced from the rhythms of natural experience, a dissociation of the cognitive self from the somatic self that has tremendous consequences. As Gandhi lamented, the music of the mind is in danger of drowning out the music of the universe. This is reflected in postmodern ideas that posit that "it's all made up," that there's no reality outside of language, that the best we can do is be self-conscious, self-referential, and witty. If we really believe that nothing exists outside our language (especially when we regard language as primarily verbal), we'll probably be compelled to talk even more and listen even less. The spiral of loneliness and despair spins another rotation. We no longer listen to artists such as Arthur Schnabel, the pianist, who remarked, "The notes I handle no better than many pianists. But the pauses between the notes—ah, that is where the art presides!"

We see the psychology of consumerism/materialism at work in therapy in a number of ways. One is the disconnection of language from felt experience. A distinguishing feature of a symptom is that what is said or thought doesn't seem to affect what is done or felt. A person says, "I want this to happen," but it doesn't happen. The impotence of language—when words are neither injunctive nor evocative—reflects its disconnection from the realities of both the somatic self and the relational field. In self-relations terms, essen has no fressen. It has no pulse, no beat, no rhythm, or connection to felt experience. It doesn't properly name or correlate with the reality of the present moment. As language becomes self-contained and indifferent to reality, reality becomes indifferent to the speaker of the language. A person senses that "nothing makes a difference" and collapses into depression or cynicism. The image becomes all and suffering deepens.

The addiction of consumerism gnaws at our national (and increasingly, our world) soul. The rhythms of television, automobiles, and computers disconnect us further from the natural rhythms of heartbeats, breath, and feeling. Our connection to the pulse of life has been loosened, and a feeling of desperate emptiness grows more ominous. The self is thought of as isolated, waiting to be filled and fulfilled by the right product. Therapy is often sought after and conducted in these terms, an attempted solution that affirms the problem.

In such situations, love is regarded as sentimental and sappy. Love as courage or as a relational skill is overlooked. Love of self and other as a mature, tender, and rigorous discipline goes unnoticed. When we hold too loose, the experience of life—of oneself or an other—sifts through our fingers, like sand. We are left grasping at images, clutching shadows, growing weaker on what T. S. Eliot called "the bitter subsistence on shadow fruit." We long for what the poet Robert Bly (1986) intimated in saying,

> And we did what we did, made love attentively, then
> dove into the river, and our bodies joined as calmly
> as the swimmer's shoulders glisten at dawn,
> as the pine tree stands in the rain at the edge of the village.
> The affection rose on a slope century after century.
>
> And one day my faithfulness to you was born.

For a deeper understanding of this faithfulness and affection, we turn our attention now to the empathic connection of the relational self.

Not too tight, not too loose: The felt connection of the relational self

> There are two types of truth. In the shallow type, the opposite of a true statement is false. In the deeper kind, the opposite of a true statement is equally true.
>
> —Neils Bohr

Occupying the two extremes of relatedness, the contracted tightness of fundamentalism and the loose depression of consumerism have much in common. Both are ideologies that take one away from being present in the moment. Both are disconnected from, and hostile to, the nature of the body and the environment. A person's primary relationship is not to life, but to text or image. (In fundamentalism, the text remains the same; in consumerism, the images are forever changing.) This disconnection from human and natural relatedness encourages further violence, apathy, depression, fear, and isolation.

Self-relations psychotherapy is an exploration of how such suffering may be relieved through relational connections. In terms of the interconnected circles of Figure 2.1, it emphasizes the entire figure—me, you, us, and the field—as the basic unit of knowing. As we will see, the relationship may be an intrapersonal one—such as between the somatic self and the cognitive self—or an interpersonal one. The basic idea is that when the self holds differences—and this is quite a skill to cultivate—good things happen. An experience of what Maureen O'Hara (1996) calls *relational empathy* develops, involving the capacity to sense a field that holds and supports the different truths or experiences in relationship.

A basic premise of this relational knowing is that multiple truths exist simultaneously. When the relational connections between these truths is lost, bad things tend to happen. Stated more formally:

1. The problem is not the problem. The problem is that what is pointed to as the problem is disconnected from its relational context and from its relational others.
2. To dissolve a problem, bring it back into relational connection.

For example, say the person holds the idea, "Life sucks." How do you respond to such a statement? Do you agree or disagree? Self-relations suggests that such a statement is true, as true as the opposite truth that life is incredibly beautiful. It is precisely the sustained disconnection of one truth from its complement that makes for a troubled view. When this imbalance is maintained, the need to control arises and a problem-defined self appears. We will see how self-relations works to dissolve the problem by (1) validating the position the person is identified with (e.g., life sucks), (2) activating and holding the complementary truth or position (life is beautiful), and then (3) finding a way to feel both at the same time.

In a relational approach, the image or text is not primary. God has many faces: *self can be imaged in many ways, but self is no image.* Self is not a "thing," but a context and a relational process. The consciousness that feels and sees (and is felt and seen) through images and descriptions to a deeper pattern that connects is more basic. Thus, the identity question is answered not in terms of "I am the follower of orthodox images" or "I am the consumer of life" but, rather, "I am (with you) the consciousness that experiences multiple truths." Because self arises from relationship, it is fluid and context-sensitive. It is therefore difficult to describe in literal or scientific language, for it is not a fixed thing. Because its face and form are changing, poetic and relational languages are sometimes more helpful in describing it.

If the self is indeed fluid and its forms ever-changing, its principles and ethics are especially important. The key ethical principle for a relational self is the loving sponsorship of life in all forms. This would include the golden rule of doing unto others as you would have them do unto you, as well as the vow of loving both oneself and others (including enemies) with all one's heart, soul, and mind. It includes commitments to tolerance, humility, deep listening, centering, compassionate action, and nonviolence. It might include cultivating what Gary Snyder (in Carolan, 1996) has called the "wild mind":

> It means self-organizing. . . . It means elegantly self-disciplining, self-regulating, self-maintained. That's what wilderness is. Nobody has to do the management plan for it. So I say to people, let's trust in the self-disciplined elegance of wild mind. Practically speaking, a life that is vowed to simplicity, appropriate boldness, good humor, gratitude, unstinted work and play, and lots of walking, brings us close to the actually existing world and its wholeness. (p. 24)

Drawing from another tradition, it might include commitments to avoid the seven "deadly sins" of pride, greed, lust, anger, gluttony, envy, and sloth. The idea of "sin" is taken here in its etymological sense of the Greek archery term meaning "off-center" or an arrow that "misses the mark." Thus, we are not emphasizing either traditional morality or guilt-inducing fundamentalisms, but terms that may help a person to notice when his actions are disconnected from his center and his relatedness to others. Since the persistence of such actions usually leads to ineffective suffering (precisely because they are nonrelational and thus isolating), their detection can help a person "let go" and "return to center" in a way that allows a reconnection with the relational self. The point is to neither shut out nor get caught in, say, anger, but to be with it relationally and "sponsor" it in ways that transform it.

Another perspective on the relational self was offered by Gandhi. Shortly before his assassination, he gave his grandson, Arun, a talisman upon which were engraved "Seven Blunders." Gandhi believed that it is out of these blunders that violence emerges and infects the world. The blunders are:

- wealth without work
- pleasure without conscience
- knowledge without character
- commerce without morality
- science without humanity
- worship without sacrifice
- politics without principles

Gandhi called these imbalances "passive violence." He maintained that passive violence feeds the active violence which is rampant in our world. Violent acts of war, crime and rebellion sprout from the roots of passive violence. He also believed that efforts to achieve peace would be fruitless as long as we ignore the passive violence in our midst.

The relational self involves a commitment to overcome the passive violence of everyday living. The experience of the relational self is evident in many contexts. One of Gregory Bateson's (1955/1972) great insights was that the simultaneous holding of multiple frames or truths underlies all distinctly human experiences, such as intimacy, play, hypnosis, mythology, and psychopathology. We can translate this observation into the following principle:

> *To generate a nonrational state of consciousness (love, intimacy, humor, pathology, trance, symptoms, play, etc.), activate two seemingly contradictory truths or experiences simultaneously.*

In intimacy, for example, once we get beyond the romantic ideal of $1 + 1 = 1$, where differences are obliterated, we see a more mature version of $1 + 1 = 3$, where the differences of "I" and "thou" held in a unified field of consciousness give birth to a third shared "us."

Another example of relational logic is humor, where the punch line opens an unexpected (and funny) frame of reference to hold besides the expected one. Thus, relational logic is part of a Marxist theory of consciousness, with Groucho being its chief spokesperson. Groucho Marx was one of the great masters at expanding beyond a single frame of reference. He was especially terrific when seducing and cajoling the fundamentalist rich socialite played by the actress Margaret Dumont. In one scene, he was making suggestive remarks about coming up to her room that night. She harumphed and exclaimed, "Well, that is a lot of innuendo." In his inimitable way, Groucho replied "Well, I'll be in yer window and out yer window before you know it!" The relational logic of "innuendo" and "in yer window" momentarily liberates consciousness from the dreary tyranny of a single literal view of life.

Later we will see how shifts in identity engender the need to hold opposite or multiple frames simultaneously—the death of an old identity and the birth of a new identity—and examine further how altered states of consciousness are inevitable at this time. We will also see how these altered states are symptomatic or therapeutic, depending on whether the opposites are regarded as complementary or as irreconcilable and whether a relational field (e.g., love) is felt to underlie and imbue both simultaneously. For now I would like to simply suggest that self-relations is a relational approach to identity that seeks to see or feel through different images to what T. S. Eliot has called "a further union, a deeper communion."[6] In holding multiple images or descriptions simultaneously, one is freed from what Bateson (1970/1972) described as the pathology of operating from a single position. Life begins to flow through a person's consciousness again, thereby allowing positions, images, and texts to change. A renewed body-mind connection develops, and the problem-defined self gives way to the relational self.

The relational self is able to attend with tender sobriety to each changing moment, for it is based on neither repression nor consumerism. Being centered and grounded yet not fixed in a rigid position, the self develops greater potency and presence. The capacity for mature love is more apparent, and the skills of nonviolence and sponsorship may be developed. Principles and practices for cultivating these skills of love are the focus for the remainder of the book.

Summary

We have described the journey through life in terms of relational cycles. In a given cycle, a person starts with a perspective or position ("self"), then notices and includes a different perspective or position ("other"), then experiences a relational self as the conversation between the differences, and finally experiences an integration into a larger field of spirit or love. The cycle is repeated over and over again, with different sets of psychological truths or experiences, thereby allowing for a gradual realization that the Kingdom of God is within.

A person's quality of attention is a major factor in these processes. Holding too tight, a person may fall prey to the fear and furies of fundamentalism, where the other is regarded as irreversi-

---

[6] This notion of "seeing through" images was crucial to James Joyce's (1916) theory of aesthetics (see Osbon, 1991, pp. 246–248). Building on the work of Thomas Aquinas, Joyce argued that there are two types of art, improper (or kinetic) and proper (or static). In improper art, such as advertising or pornography, the intent of the artist is to pull a person's attention away from himself and lock it inside the content of the frame. A state of agitation (desire or repulsion) results, with compulsive behavior (e.g., buy the product) being suggested as the way out of the agitation. In proper art, a person's attention is guided through the frame, to feel some beauty or goodness that cannot be framed. The resulting state is quietude and centeredness. In the age of television consciousness and pop culture, it seems very little of this crucial art of "seeing through" is being practiced, with disastrous consequences.

bly separate and dangerous to oneself. Holding too loose, a person may become self-absorbed and indifferent to others, thereby slipping into the abyss of addiction to cynical and empty consumerism. When the person holds "not too tight, not too loose," the relational empathy and paradoxical logic of love as a skill may be cultivated.

A person, of course, may shift between these different relational approaches. Fundamentalism may reign at one point, and consumerism at another. When a person becomes identified with either style, problems are likely to develop. The rest of the book is devoted to elaborating how the self-relations approach may be helpful in resolving such problems.

3

THE RELATIONAL SELF

IDENTITY, PROBLEM FORMATION, AND
PROBLEM RESOLUTION

How did the world begin? For Jewish mystics the world began with an act of withdrawal. God did *tzimtzum*. God contracted God's self to leave space for the world to exist. Before that God was everywhere, filling every space and every dimension. After this *tzimtzum*—this withdrawal—some divine energy entered the emerging world, but this divine light, this divine energy was too strong, overpowering the worlds that tried to contain it, and the universe exploded with a cosmic bang. Shards of divine light, of holiness, were scattered everywhere in the universe. The sparks of holiness are often buried deep in the cosmic muck of the universe, they are difficult to behold and yet they are everywhere, in everyone, in every situation. They are the life and meaning of the universe.

We live in this world of shattering. We feel in our bodies and in our souls the brokenness of the world, we too feel at times the resonance in our selves of that initial cosmic shattering. Our bodies, like that primordial world, try not to contain, but rather to hold onto the divine light and energy flowing around us and in us. But, as in the world's origin, our bodies are too frail, made only frailer with the passage of time, and so we begin to leak our divine image/energy. Perhaps then illness is really the leaking of our souls. In this world of shattered hopes and expectations, we search for wholeness.

Moses, as you know, shattered the first set of tablets, the first set of the Ten Commandments. And then he got a second set that he helped to write. When the ark was constructed for the sanctuary, the rabbis tell us not only the whole second set of tables was put into the holy ark, but the pieces of the first set as well.

Wholeness comes not from ignoring the broken pieces, or hoping to magically glue them back together.

The shattered co-exists with the whole, the divine is to be found amidst the darkest depths and the heaviest muck of the universe.

Every moment has the potential for redemption and wholeness. Our brokenness gives us that vision and the potential to return some of the divine sparks scattered in the world.

—*A version of* Kavanah
(a Jewish reading of intentionality),
by Rabbi Michael Strassfeld

THIS CHAPTER examines the relational self as a simultaneous experience of wholeness and parts. The first section describes the three basic aspects of the relational self: (1) a center of consciousness in the somatic self, (2) a psychological relationship in the cognitive self, and (3) a field of awareness in the relational self. We will see how these distinctions correspond with the three principles of beingness, relatedness, and belongingness, and how sustained "breaks" in these levels of self underlie symptomatic behavior. The second section offers a more specific model for how this occurs and suggests three intervention principles for beginning to repair relational "breaks."

A question of identity: Who are you?

As a young boy growing up in an Irish Catholic alcoholic family, I got into quite a bit of trouble. Often this would culminate with my father's cornering me and asking, with furious (and often inebriated) intensity, *Who the hell do you think you are anyway?* This question has stuck in my mind over the years, prompting a variety of answers, as well as different approaches to asking the question.

The question of identity is central to psychotherapy. Clients are

TABLE 3.1. PRINCIPLES OF THE RELATIONAL SELF

Principle of:	Experienced as:	Self-relations term
Beingness	felt center in body	somatic self
Belongingness	expanded feeling of belonging to field	relational self
Relatedness	connection, interaction, mental differences	cognitive self

answering the question in some way that doesn't fit external challenges or have internal resonance, giving rise to sustained suffering. For example, a person holding the identity, "I am depression," will find it hard to connect with aspects of her knowledge that are outside of this description. As therapists we are forever curious about how a person may hold and respond to the identity question in fresh and helpful ways.

From a relational point of view, identity is not fixed or reducible to an image. It is a contextual experience that is ever-changing. Thus, self-relations sees the "self" not as a static form but as an experience of three distinct principles. Table 3.1 shows these principles, along with the ways in which they are commonly experienced. We will examine each principle in turn.

1. Self as a center of consciousness: The principle of beingness

> God is in me or
> else is not at all.
>
> —*Wallace Stevens*

This first premise is meant as an alternative to the three major causal metaphors used in psychotherapy, namely that (1) you are your past (personal history), (2) you are your biology, or (3) you are your social context (ethnicity, gender, family, etc.). Self-relations acknowledges that these are immensely important factors in

---

TABLE 3.2. PREMISES OF THE PRINCIPLE OF BEINGNESS

1. The beingness of life is distinctively present in each person.
2. When the direct experience of beingness is ignored, denied, or cursed in a person, symptoms are likely to develop.
3. To alleviate symptoms and relieve suffering, reawaken and cultivate awareness of the basic goodness of being in a person.

---

shaping your experience and that you must come to terms with each of them. Like money in modern times, ignoring them is the kiss of death. But if you make any of them primary, you'll also go down. So while respecting the importance of personal history, biology, and social place, self-relations says that you're something more: you are a one-of-a-kind being of consciousness.

This can be expressed as *the principle of beingness*. Its form is represented in Figure 3.1 by a simple circle, to indicate an existence ("ex" = "stand," to stand out). The point is, you really do exist as a human being. You have a center, a core of being that is blessed. To forget or ignore this leads to great suffering.

This may sound a bit esoteric, so let me give a few simple examples. If you were to meet my young daughter Zoe, I could say to you, "Behold Zoe consciousness!" and you would get it. You would get that she's no story, she's no description—she's

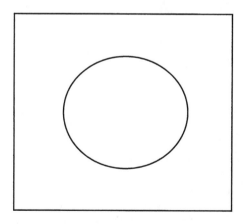

FIGURE 3.1. A BEING IS DISTINGUISHED IN CONSCIOUSNESS

consciousness itself, she's the real thing! Or, if you've ever had the privilege of sitting with a person dying, you likely felt a deep consciousness in his or her process of letting go. A client of mine recently spoke of her struggle to come to terms with her dying father. He had been a terribly abusive man all her life, violating her in many ways. She broke off contact with him for years, but visited him upon hearing that he was dying of cancer. When she saw him on his deathbed, she was shocked to see that his mask of hatred and violence had dissolved, and a gentle lonely man was exposed. She described it like the scene at the end of *Return of the Jedi,* when Darth Vader ("Dark Father") is unmasked to reveal his atrophied human face. Her heart opened but her body and behavior were still paralyzed by what had happened over the years. In the therapy session she struggled to reconcile the lifelong image of her father and her recent experiential sensing of the consciousness behind the image.

In a similar way, we all become caught in fixed images or static stories that obscure and deny the dynamic life force pulsating through everything. It is easy to become seduced into locking onto the image and more difficult to feel through it to the self as consciousness. But I believe this is one of our challenges as therapists, to sense and reconnect consciousness to itself.

The experience of beingness is cultivated through an awareness of a center within the somatic self. The idea of a center is central to many cultures. Malidoma Somé, an African Dagara who was kidnapped by the Jesuits and raised to be a priest, escaped from his captors in late adolescence and returned to his people. There was great concern in the village because he had not undergone the rite of passage crucial to his culture. It was finally decided that he could undergo the ritual with the younger boys. Somé (1994) describes the initial instructions given by the ritual elder:

> Somehow what he said did not sound strange to me or—I found out later—to anyone. It was as if he were putting into words something we all knew, something we had never questioned and could never verbalize.
> What he said was this: The place where he was standing was the center. Each one of us possessed a center that he had grown away from after birth. To be born was to lose contact with our center, and to grow from childhood to adulthood was to walk

away from it. "The center is both within and without. It is everywhere. But we must realize it exists, find it, and be with it, for without the center we cannot tell who we are, where we come from, and where we are going."

He explained that the purpose of Baor (the initiation process) was to find our center. This school specialized in repairing the wear and tear incurred in the course of thirteen rainy seasons of life. I was twenty. Had I been home all that time, I would have gone through this process seven years ago. I wondered if I was catching up too late but then thought, better late than never.

"No one's center is like someone else's. Find your own center, not the center of your neighbor; not the center of your father or mother or family or ancestor but that center which is yours and yours alone." (pp. 198–199)

The experience of a center is first awakened through such rituals or through blessings from special people. Most people can remember someone in their lives—a family member, teacher, friend—who really saw them as special and unique. These are not intellectual events: they are about seeing and calling forth the spirit of life that infuses each person. Blessings are crucial acts in the awakening of each person to herself and to the world. Without them, love and other skillful human acts are not possible.

The opposite of a blessing is a curse. Curses are prominent in most traumatic events, which are the forerunners of many symptoms. A trauma typically involves not only a physical violation, but also a curse where the perpetrator invades and imprints life-denying ideas like "you exist only to serve me," "you are stupid," "you deserve to be punished," "you are unlovable," and so forth. Self-relations refers to these events as acts of negative sponsorship wherein alien ideas are planted in a person. These alienating ideas represent a sort of autoimmune disease in the "psychological immune system" needed to differentiate what's "me" from what's "alien" to me. In other words, violence tears the "sheathing" that surrounds a person, and through the tear rush the aliens.[1] If such

---

[1] The sheathing that surrounds each being can be seen graphically in the response of young children to strangers or unfamiliar situations. A three-year-old may be exuberant and completely outgoing while playing at home with her friends or family, but grow shy and hide behind her parent's protective body while sizing up a stranger. Because a child's sheathing is so delicate, a parent is responsible for shielding it from events that might tear it. This is what I mean by "a tear in the sheathing."

violence is not acknowledged and healed, a person comes to misidentify with these alienating ideas as herself and to act accordingly. Self-relations looks to discriminate alienating ideas from self-affirming ones, and suggests methods by which a person may "externalize" these aliens and reconnect with internally resonant descriptions (cf. White & Epston, 1990).

Children initially rely exclusively on blessings from others to realize their beingness. But with maturity we develop the possibility of cultivating our beingness via self-generated means. Self-relations refers to such methods as self-sponsorship practices and is interested in identifying the ones that work for a given person. One example of self-sponsorship is centering practices—such as walking, meditating, talking to a friend, art—that reconnect a person to a calm, non-intellectual center of being. They touch the tender soft spot and allow new confidence and deeper relatedness. Through a combination of blessings and centering practices, a person may resist the curses of alienation and recover the primacy of beingness.

Another example of self-sponsorship is in relation to one's suffering. Self-relations assumes that suffering is a major way in which life awakens within a person. Something is trying to wake up, but it needs human presence and sponsorship to be realized. Unfortunately, most of our cultural practices emphasize avoidance or numbing of suffering, based on the belief that it cannot be transformed and thus touching it will make things worse. Self-relations emphasizes that perhaps the greatest gift of human consciousness is the capacity to transform experience. Thus, we look to develop ways to accept and attend to symptoms as gifts, albeit often "terrible gifts" that we would not will upon our worst enemies. We practice accepting such gifts as means to realize a deeper understanding and connection to self and world.

2. Self as relational field: The principle of belongingness

> The unity is to be seen: afterwards, all the differences. This is the function of the poet.
>
> —R. H. Blyth, 1991

There is no place in this new kind of physics both for the field and matter, for the field is the only reality.

—*Albert Einstein, in Capek, 1961, p. 319*

The separateness apparent in the world is secondary. Beyond the world of opposites is an unseen, but experienced unity and identity in us all.

—*Joseph Campbell, in Osbon, 1991, p. 25*

We noted in Chapter 1 that there exists an intelligence greater than the individual. In self-relations we emphasize this as the experience of a non-local relational self. Such an experience is readily familiar to most people, though typically it is not talked about much, especially in terms of how it may be used in difficult challenges. To get a sense of where a person experiences a relational self, one can ask:

1. When do you feel most like yourself?
2. When you need to reconnect with yourself, what do you do?
3. When is life not a problem for you?

Typical responses might include playing or listening to music, going for a walk, being in nature, talking with good friends, reading, meditating, conscious breathing, knitting, performing art, dancing, spending time with one's family, and so forth. These activities may be regarded as *ordinary experiences of self-transcendence.* They are everyday ways in which a person connects with a presence greater than herself, while keeping and even deepening a connection to her center at the same time. If asked to describe what existential or phenomenological shifts occur during such events, most people report decreased internal dialogue, timelessness, and an expansion of a felt sense of self. A person feels more confident and secure in this state, with a decreased emphasis on being "in control." If you ask where the sense of self ends during such experiences, people will look at you quizzically, because no sharp boundary exists. *This expanded feeling of self beyond boundaries of skin and either-or ideology, while maintaining a center, is the experience of self as a relational field.* It joins a

TABLE 3.3. PREMISES OF THE PRINCIPLE OF
BELONGINGNESS

1. A person belongs to (or is part of) a larger relational field.
2. When a person experiences a sustained "break in belonging" to the relational field, symptoms are likely to develop.
3. To relieve suffering and reconcile symptomatic conflict, awaken awareness of the intelligence of the relational field.

person to herself as well as to others, allowing connections at intrapersonal, interpersonal, and (often) transpersonal levels.

The experience of a relational field is described by *the principle of belonginess*. This relationship is represented in the traditional figure/ground or figure/field diagram shown in Figure 3.2. The relational field may be experienced as spiritual (I belong to a higher power, and he/she/it moves through me); organismic (I belong to nature, and it moves through me); social (I belong to my marriage/family/culture/community, and it permeates and supports my consciousness); or psychological (my experience/perspective is embedded within a larger field of experiences/memories/archetypes, and they guide/inform me). For a given person, there may be multiple experiences, and even multiple levels, of

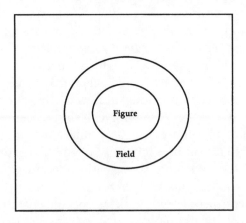

FIGURE 3.2. EACH DISTINCTION OF CONSCIOUSNESS BELONGS
TO A LARGER FIELD

the relational self. The relational self is non-local; it is not a "thing" located within any physical person, place or thing. It is the field that holds persons, places, and things in living interconnectedness. This field can be felt, understood, and used in many, many ways.

The important observation, for our purposes, is that the self-transcendent experience of the relational field is present when life is working for a person, when life is not defined or perceived as a problem. Conversely, a person struggling with a symptom has experienced a "break in belonging" to the field; she doesn't feel a sense of connection to, or communion with, a power or presence greater than herself. The experience of self is contracted and split, and the unified field supporting self and others is not felt. This cut-off from context leads to identification with the intellect and its fear-driven strategies of control and domination (and experiences of being out of control and reactive), rather than curiosity and connectedness. Again, this is the basis for fundamentalism and other forms of alienation and violence.

The disconnection from the relational field occurs in many ways, most of them involuntary. Some disconnections are the healthy first steps to individuation, as when an adolescent rebels from her family. Thus, breaks in belonging are not necessarily bad; they are inevitable steps of separation that are hopefully followed by a reunion with the field, on terms and understandings more helpful to the person. But some experiences—such as traumas—don't allow such reconnection to occur. If the conditions of violence or trauma prevail, a sustained break occurs in which the person or experience is split off from the larger relational fields.

Connection to a relational field usually enhances personal agency, though this is not always the case. As Wilber (1995) lucidly notes, two problems may occur in the relationship between the local (individual) self and the non-local (relational field) self. First, a person may lose connection to the larger field and get locked into "agency without communion" (or isolated dominance), where she thinks of herself as the ultimate power or intelligence. This is a lonely, impotent place where control and domination are the best one can hope for. Second, a person may merge with the field and develop "communion without agency" (or codependency), in which her individual center is lost. This is also a lonely place, where a person hopes to be rescued or healed by others.

In the healthy sense of "agency with communion," a person feels both her center and a connection to the relational field. They are complementary sources of guidance and intelligence, on either side of the cognitive self; that is, the mind is the middle ground between the inner center and the outer field. One of its major functions is to ensure that communion with the relational field does not disintegrate one's center, but connects it with additional perspectives and resources.

The thirst to connect with the relational field is unquenchable (Fromm, 1956). In this regard, a number of psychological symptoms are seen in part as unsuccessful attempts to return to the field. A person may try to reunite with the field by ignoring or abusing herself. For example, an addiction—whether to drugs or alcohol, food, sex, bad relationships, or cults—is initially a hopeful experience of losing oneself to a "higher power." The addictive agent—the drug, the person, the guru—is a sort of false sponsor that promises an experience of the relational field. However, the price a person must pay is disrespect and abuse of herself. Thus, when she gets there the result is emptiness, depression, and self-hatred. Because the need is strong and the initial promise and experience was so seductive, the person thinks maybe she didn't give/take/do enough. This begins a downward spiral of more self-destructive activities, with increasingly empty results.

In this way, one part of the symptom is an attempt to return to the relational self, while another is a reenactment of the self-destructive violence that exiled one from the larger self in the first place. For example, a person taking drugs hopes they will remove her isolation and anxiety, but they actually deepen them. The absence of love in the false sponsorship given by the drugs matches the absence of love in her previous human sponsors.

Thus, a major focus of self-relations is to help the person satisfy her attempt to return to the field, but through self-loving rather than self-destructive means. As we will see in the next chapter, much of this involves nonverbal bodymind practices. For example, in any performance art—dance, music, acting, aikido, sculpting, writing—one will hear from the artist the importance of "relaxing" and feeling the rhythm. This is a disciplined and rigorous process that allows a deeper connection to the relational field from which new possibilities arise. In psychotherapy we help clients do this via many relational methods, including joining and validating experience, entraining with a client's rhythms, encouraging centering and a felt sense of experience, and so forth. Disciplines such as prayer and meditation, service, and other mindfulness practices may also be helpful for some clients.

In exploring the experience of a relational field, we remember that there are many ways to know it. A person's sense of a "higher power" is her own. For one person it may be the experience of being at the ocean, for another it may be felt while holding her child. Another person might know it when involved in a meditation community, another in political activism. At the same time, the field itself cannot be reduced to any description. So while a person may activate the relational field in a particular way, she may then learn how to work within the field in a more general way.

For example, a senior partner in a law firm was struggling with her work situation. Every time she attended a meeting with her partners, an argument would break out in which she would lose her cool. One way to understand this is that stress contracts one's attention, leading to a "break in belonging" to the relational field that might provide some guidance. To reinstate the relational field, one can use any experience in which a person has felt it. The lawyer knew the relational field when she sang opera at home. As we examined this experience, she described a connection to a vibrant, beautiful energy that surrounded her when she sang. Examining this energy further, it became clear that it was not tied to any content of the musical experience. Rather, it was a living presence that imbued and surrounded the musical experience, providing nurturance, strength, intuitive direction, and centering. We explored how she might feel this "field presence" in the office, how it might be sensed while we talked about the problem, and how it could be evoked when she was in her office meetings. As she later reported, her capacity to tap into and sustain a connection with the relational field made a big difference in her navigation through the next meetings. It led to her effectively addressing the relational dynamics of the senior partners in ways that led to significant changes. Thus, the experience of a relational field may be known through certain experiences, but may be used in any circumstance.

3. Self as relational differences: The principle of relatedness

So far we have seen two different non-cognitive ways a person has of knowing self and life: the vibrant center and felt sense of beingness at one's core, and the expansive feeling of communion with a field and intelligence larger than oneself. This in effect suggests two buffers for the cognitive self: the center and the field. *An experience of all three is crucial for the relational self.*

As we noted earlier, the first two goals of sponsorship are to awaken a sense of self and awaken a sense of the world. The third principle of sponsorship is to introduce practices by which a person may navigate between these two domains to realize a self-in-world and a world-in-self. (As Christ pointed out, the Kingdom of God is within.) *These are the main functions of the cognitive self: to sponsor experience and to develop relatedness between different selves.*

The *cognitive self* is the basic, everyday sense of self that most people have when life is not a problem. It is socially constructed, based on the person's present age and social identity, and is centered in the head. It includes competencies, resources, associations with present social others, skills, and multiple perspectives. It uses frames and models to make meaning, plan, evaluate, and otherwise try to manage the world of experience. In a symptom, this sense of self disappears, contracts, dissociates, or is otherwise nullified. Some clients will talk about just wanting to get back to this "normal" self.

The cognitive self is also the medium between self and world. Its major language is relational differences: different positions, different truths, different people, different times or places, different values, and so on. In contrast to a center and the field, it is forever confronted with differences and the task of how to correlate these differences to develop an effective community. As Bateson (1979) repeatedly emphasized, *mind is relationship and dif-*

TABLE 3.4. THE PREMISES OF THE PRINCIPLE OF
RELATEDNESS

1. A person realizes her self through conversations of relational
   differences.
2. When a "break in relatedness" persists, the experience of self
   disappears, the fundamentalist ego-mind reigns, and
   symptoms are likely to arise.
3. To reduce suffering and reconcile symptoms, reestablish a
   conversation between different positions of identity.

ference is the basic unit of mind. Thus, the challenge of the
cognitive self may be described in terms of *the principle of relatedness*. Its form is represented by the two interconnected circles of Figure 3.3. In terms of psychological identity, the principle
of relatedness may be described in terms of a subject/object relationship, in which the person is identified with one position—the
subject, or what we might call the "me" position—while directing her attention to another position—the object, or what we
might call the "not-me" position. Thus, the cognitive self is a
pattern of me/not-me connections occurring within a relational
field.

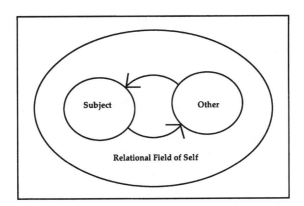

FIGURE 3.3. THE RELATIONAL SELF AS THE PATTERN THAT
CONNECTS THE DIFFERENCES

This me/not-me relationship may be expressed with just about any distinction. Some relational distinctions relevant to psychotherapy include:

> self (me, us, I)/other (you, them, it)
> good/bad
> power/love
> interior/exterior
> masculine/feminine
> field/center
> individual/collective
> healthy/sick
> problem/solution
> therapist/client
> life/death
> thinking/feeling
> mind/body
> conscious/unconscious

The challenge is what to make of these differences. Is one forever "better" or more important than the other? Can they touch and transform each other? Is each distinction in fact contained in its opposite, so that one's enemy *is* oneself? Is there a unitive field that holds these dualities? Can differences be honored, even as community is realized? These are just a few of the crucial questions regarding the cognitive self and the ubiquitous differences that it faces.

Self-relations suggests that in healthy situations, these relational differences operate in a conversational connectedness, the sort of "I-thou" relationship described by Martin Buber (1923/1958). In intimacy, there is an experience of a "me," a "you," and the relational self of "us" that is felt when both the "I" and "thou" are validated. The experience of therapeutic trance (Gilligan, 1987) reflects a similar "self/(other) self" relatedness. The fictional terms of "conscious" and "unconscious" are provided, the suggestions to do something while just letting it happen ("your hand can lift involuntarily") are given, and the resulting experience of "it's happening but I'm not making it happen" (e.g., my hand is lifting, but it's old Mr. or Ms. NOT-ME that's lifting it!) is central to every hypnotic happening.

An exceptional example of how this relational process happens in art was given by the Chilean writer Isabel Allende. In an interview with Michael Toms (1994), she described how the characters in her novels first appear as "beings in her belly." For months she lovingly holds these beings in a sort of pregnancy. Then, on her mother's birthday (to honor her mother, who is also her editor!), she creates a ritual ceremony wherein the beings move from her belly into her awareness. As they emerge, she follows three rules: fall in love with them on their own terms, accurately describe them (as they appear, not as she would like them to appear), and describe the relationships that occur among them. (How much this sounds like good parenting!) In the first stage of the process, these beings in the belly are guiding the story; in the second stage of editing, her writer's ear and craft are more active. *In both stages, the creative relational self emerges from the conversation between the different selves: the archetypal process of the somatic self and the sponsorship capacities of the cognitive self.*

The above examples suggest that relatedness between differences is played out in different fields. Relational differences require a relational field as a container or, as Jung described it, a "temenos."[2] The container for mental differences may be intrapersonal or interpersonal; or it could be the individual, the marriage, the family, or a larger community. Without the durable strength of such a container, the differences will remain unintegrated. Thus, a relational field is crucial to develop in order to resolve conflict.

For therapy purposes, self-relations generally emphasizes three types of relational connections needed for learning and development. The first is the *interpersonal,* involving the "I" and the "thou" (Buber, 1923/1958). When connections between self and others are polarized or isolated—me vs. you, us against them—problems get worse and the possibility of violence increases. The second is the *embodied intrapersonal,* a felt sense of vertical re-

---

[2] In ancient Greece, a temenos was an altar or place of rest where a person could receive spiritual nourishment and guidance. Later, alchemists used the term to describe the container that held the different metals transmuted into the alchemical gold. The container needed to be strong enough to withstand enormous heat. Jung used the term in the latter sense, suggesting that relationships such as marriage and therapy constituted temenonic fields that allowed the different elements of the soul to heat up and be transformed.

latedness between the cognitive/social self in the "head" and the emotional/archetypal self in "the belly." The third is also intrapersonal, a horizontal *interhemispheric relatedness* required for experience to be processed and integrated (cf. Rossi, 1977; Shapiro, 1995). Self-relations posits that a sustained "break in relatedness" in any of these domains will result in a "frozen in time" consciousness that is unable to learn and thus likely to produce symptoms.

In problem situations, relatedness between different positions is denied or ignored. (As Krishnamurti used to say, the whole misery of mankind lies in the gap between the subject and the object.) An interpersonal "thou" becomes an objectified "it," and the "beings in the belly" are reduced to an inhuman other (e.g., depression or anxiety) to be removed by any means necessary.

Life moves through us as we move through it. In the cognitive self, this is represented by a series of progressive experiences.[3] The key is to find ways to respect and value each experience in its ever-changing forms. This is a difficult process, as anyone ever involved in an intimate relationship will readily admit. *It requires a centering within one's beingness, an openness to the relational field, and a willingness and ability to dialogue.* Even under the best conditions, imperfection reigns. As Bill Wilson (1967), the founder of Alcoholics Anonymous, noted:

> This is no success story in the ordinary sense of the word. It is a story of suffering transmuted, under grace, into gradual spiritual progress. (p. 35)

As we come back to relatedness, our experience of self as dialogue develops. Holding the tension between differences nurtures a deeper harmony and capacity to act with love and integrity. If we remain faithful to the conversation, at some point what Jung (1916/1971) termed the "transcendent function" occurs: the opposites integrate into a united form, where a difficult contradic-

---

[3] This is not a linear development: it is more a progressive spiral of developmental cycles. Each cycle has a beginning, a middle, and an end. For example, a long marriage may have four or five developmental cycles over its course. Each cycle has its unique experiences and challenges. Also, each part of the cycle has it own types of experiences; for example, the end of a cycle often includes more experiences of loss and cognitive impotence. This is often when clients come to see therapists.

tion transforms into a graceful integration. The differences are now seen as essential complements, and a deeper sense of unity is felt. Jung described this process wherein differences move from conflict to mutual support as the central means by which the self grows. What allows this remarkable transformation to occur is, of course, the courage to love.

A self-relations model of how symptoms develop

The three principles of beingness, belongingness, and relatedness—and their corresponding experiences of a center in the somatic self, a field in the relational self, and a relational difference in the cognitive self—suggest questions that might help a person stay present and responsive:

1. Can you sense your center?
2. Can you feel a connection to a presence greater than you?
3. Can you hold the tension of the opposites and experience the conversation between differences?

Conversely, the principles suggest that symptoms reflect three types of sustained breaks: a "break in beingness" (of the goodness, gifts, and vitality of self), a "break in belonging" to the (spiritual, organismic, social, or psychological) world, and a "break in relatedness" to the "other" self.

From these premises we can build a working model for self-relations therapy. Figure 3.4a represents a healthy learning situation involving three aspects of a relational self: (1) the somatic self, (2) the cognitive self, and (3) positive sponsors. In every experience, life moves through the somatic self, bringing its fressen energies. To realize the human value of these energies, they must be sponsored and transformed into essen forms of expression. As Figure 3.4a illustrates, this sponsorship comes from two sources: the cognitive self and external sponsors. Early on, the cognitive self is barely developed, so external sponsors are especially crucial. With their blessings and support, personhood is slowly de-

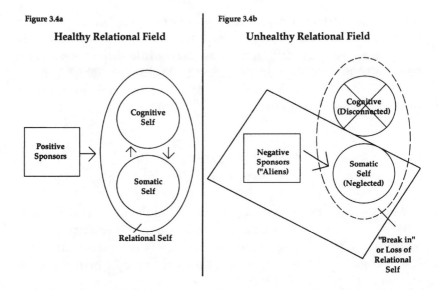

FIGURE 3.4. RELATIONAL SPACE OF THE COGNITIVE SELF, SOMATIC SELF, AND EXTERNAL SPONSORS

veloped. We still need to be seen and loved by others, but gradually we add the capacity to do it for ourselves and others as well.

Unfortunately, this developmental process may be arrested in a variety of ways. External sponsors may neglect or abuse a person. The basic message, which lacerates the bodymind and attacks the tender soft spot, is that the person is unlovable. As Figure 3.4b illustrates, a curse invades the person, causing a break in relatedness between the cognitive and somatic selves, as well as a break in belonging to the relational field. This traumatic break may not be processed, either socially (talking with others) or somatically (see Shapiro, 1995). It may be denied, minimized, repeated, rationalized, repeated, or otherwise devalued. This affirms the curse, and the person internalizes the "alien ideas" as her own.

We see this in therapy when a client says something like, "I'm really beating myself up." The therapist might ask, "Where did you ever get the idea that those are your voices?" The therapist might then share the observation that when the negative influences (e.g., hateful self-criticism) come, the person seems to have to "go away." This is done gently and sympathetically, so as to access the experience of abandonment and the feeling connected with it. The therapist might then encourage the client to note what happens to her sense of self when she comes "under the influence" of such ideas. Most clients immediately sense that they constrict, dissociate, or otherwise get smaller. The point might then be made that a basic idea in certain practices such as meditation and hypnosis is that not all ideas that move through one's mind belong to oneself. I sometimes suggest, with an Irish twinkle, that the person seems to be "possessed by aliens." I offer my opinion that listening to one's own voice should result in more presence, rather than less. This sets up a whole discussion about how to differentiate one's own voices and visions from "alien" ones that suck the life energy and self-love out of a person. Some methods for doing this are presented in Chapters 5 and 6.

While a problem-defined self misidentifies with negative sponsors, it also mistakenly disidentifies from the somatic self. In self-relations, we say that the somatic self is reduced to a "neglected self." Its contents—feelings, images, symbols—are rejected and its very presence is feared. Thus, *in a symptom a person mistakenly identifies the alien presences as her own and rejects her basic self as alien and untrustworthy.* In addition, the alien presences lead to a contraction of the cognitive self.

Thus, a problem-defined self may be said to suffer in three related ways (cf. Herman, 1992). First, the cognitive self is constricted, dissociated, fragmented, or otherwise inaccessible. When the problem comes, the cognitive self goes. Second, the somatic self is gripped in a state of "neuromuscular lock," a frozen state of fear distinguished by out-of-control emotions, hyperarousal and hypervigilance, somatization, and regression. Third, the person cannot shut out the intrusive images and voices of negative sponsors that define the self as bad, unlovable, deserving of violence, and so forth. In the language of self-relations, the cognitive self disconnects; the somatic self is neglected, literalized, and frozen into a fixed form; and negative sponsors lock into the curses and self-denigrating practices of alien presences.

This suggests the three interconnected principles of intervention listed in Table 3.5. First, therapeutic communications should access and retain the competencies, resources, and perspectives of the cognitive self. This is a crucial yet traditionally overlooked aspect of therapy. Therapy usually tunes into the neglected self

TABLE 3.5. THREE GOALS IN SELF-RELATIONS THERAPY

1. Reconnect attention to the competencies and resources of the cognitive self.
2. Access and sponsor the neglected experiences of the somatic self.
3. Reconnect awareness with its source in the relational field.

and has the therapist carry the competencies of the cognitive self. In self-relations, it is crucial that the therapist not forget that the client has many resources and competencies that are not evident when she identifies with the problem, but are nonetheless accessible.

Second, the neglected (somatic) self needs to be identified, validated, and sponsored. Much of the person's communications reveal and then conceal the experience of the tender soft spot, so it's sometimes hard to accurately sense it, name it, and begin to sponsor it in a workable way. Again, the goal in sponsoring the neglected self is to find a middle way between the extremes of disconnection (via dissociation, not listening, dominating, intellectualization, denial, projection, etc.) and indulgence (via inflation, identification, acting out, regression, sentimentality, etc.). The balance between fressen energies and essen disciplines is sought, as in the relationship of an artist to the art, or a good parent to a child.

Third, awareness of the relational field needs to be reawakened. This means identifying and removing alienating presences and reviving knowledges of the relational self. As we will see in later chapters, fighting or directly opposing the aliens is typically counterproductive. If you attack violence with violence, you will invariably get sucked up into its vortex and perpetuate the suffering. A more helpful way is for a person to first bring attention to her center. When the cognitive self touches and sponsors the somatic self, alienation is overcome and new responses become available. Simultaneously, connection to ordinary experiences of self-transcendence (walking in nature, experiencing love) can help a person connect with a presence more powerful than any alienating presence. Good examples of finding and maintaining this connection to one's center and to a relational field may be gathered from many sources, including the client's own life. One area that is especially relevant is the stories of political prisoners such as Nelson Mandela or Nathan Sharansky (1988). By examining such instances, a person begins to discover that self-love is a rigorous practice that is the most reliable antidote to overcoming repression and alienation.

To work simultaneously with these three aspects of the relational self, it is important to have an integrated, centered attention that is stable and responsive to multiple relational levels. It is equally important to develop sponsorship skills. It is to those two areas that our discussion now turns.

Summary

The most important distinction in psychological experience is the question of identity. How a person asks and answers this question constitutes the basis for much of her experience and behavior. Self-relations thinks of identity in terms of the three principles of beingness, belonginess, and relatedness. This corresponds to the experience of a somatic self and its felt center, a relational self and the experience of a field, and a cognitive self and the experience of sponsorship and integration of relational differences. That is, a person is alive, knows she is alive via a felt sense of connection to something bigger, and learns about the nature of her aliveness through encountering and eventually integrating relational differences.

On this path, development may be arrested by three types of "breaks." A break in beingness means that a person loses a felt sense of her center and consequently her sense of vitality, goodness, and unique gifts. The lights may be on, but no one seems to be home. A break in belonging means that communion with a higher power—social, spiritual, ecological—is not felt, and isolation and "agency without communion" develops. A break in relatedness means that a person identifies with one side of a distinction and refuses to acknowledge or accept the complementary distinction. This leads to recurrent conflict or withdrawal, with increasingly painful consequences.

A crucial variable is the relationship to the awakening tender soft spot of one's center. As we move through life, life moves through us with the fressen experiences of this somatic self. The blessings and guidance of a positive sponsor allows these energies to be cultivated into the essen forms of the relational self. Just as important, positive sponsorship allows the development of self-sponsorship skills.

Attacks or neglect from a negative sponsor freeze the fressen energy and disconnect it from helpful essen forms. A prolonged break between the cognitive self and somatic self develops. A symptom represents a recurrent effort for this cursed fressen energy to integrate, but each time it is rejected anew, usually due to fear or ignorance by the cognitive self or violence from external sponsors. When a symptom occurs, a person tends to lose connection with the relational field, disconnect from the competencies of the cognitive self, and become misidentified with the curses and self-denigrating practices of negative sponsors. As the fressen energies at the base of a symptomatic experience re-awaken over and over, the person devalues such experiences, thereby producing a recurrent symptom. To sponsor and transform the symptom into a valuable learning, the self-relations therapist looks to (1) reactivate the competencies of the cognitive self, (2) touch and sponsor the "neglected (somatic) self," and (3) reawaken a person's connection to the relational field.

II

PRACTICES

4

RETURN FROM EXILE

PRACTICES FOR MIND-NATURE COORDINATION

(Zen master) Basho once said to a group of students: "To learn about the pine, go to the pine. To learn about the bamboo, go to the bamboo. But this *learn* is not just what you think learn is. You only learn by becoming totally absorbed in that which you wish to learn. There are many people who think that they have learned something and willfully construct a poem which is artifice and does not flow from their delicate entrance into the life of another object."

—*Gary Snyder, 1980, p. 67*

If the therapist is trying to take a patient, give him exercises, play various propagandas on him, try to make him come over to our world for the wrong reasons, to manipulate him—then there arises a problem, a temptation to confuse the idea of manipulation with the idea of a cure. . . .

This is, I think, really what these disciplines of meditation are about. . . . They're about the problem of how to get there without getting there by the manipulative path, because the manipulative path can never get there.

—*Gregory Bateson, 1975, p. 26*

Enlightenment is an accident, but practice makes you accident-prone.

—*Richard Baker Roshi*

WALKING IN THE WOODS, or feeling the breathing and heartbeat of a loved one in our arms, we feel connected to some deeper intelligence and harmony. But when life is experienced as a problem, this natural relational field is forgotten: self and mental process are seen and experienced as separate from nature (including our bodies). The natural world is "out there," the mind is watching from the "inside," and the latter is used to dominate or control the former. But as Bateson (1979) eloquently argued, mind and nature are a necessary unity. They are different descriptions of a deep underlying wholeness.

When practices and principles regard mind and nature as separate, bad things tend to happen. Self-relations sees symptoms as arising when a person's mental processes are disconnected from his felt sense of a center and a field. In fact, a symptom is in part an attempt to repair mind-nature splits. If we can listen deeply to what the symptom is telling us, we no longer need to fear it and try (in vain) to violently destroy it.

To listen to this "other," it helps first to reconnect with the unitive field that holds both self and other. Feeling grounded and centered in this relational field, we become better able to shift attention in order to relax, focus, open, stay centered, and act decisively. We can also better recognize when we are disconnected and isolated, and then reconnect with a sense of beingness, belongingness, and relatedness.

These skills involve daily practices of attentiveness. These practices help us stabilize our attention, so that we can respond rather than react to life in each moment. In this chapter we will explore four general methods: (a) breathing awareness and muscle relaxation, (b) dropping or centering attention, (c) opening attention to the field, and (d) cleansing the doors of perception. The general idea is that as bodymind coordination is developed, ideology and rigid understandings fade. As essen awareness and fressen energy integrate, the neuromuscular lock that is at the core of symptomatic behavior loosens, and healing and the alleviation of suffering become possible. A person becomes more responsive and less reactive, more flexible and less rigid, more tuned in and less disconnected and isolated.

Given the value of these skills, the therapist is encouraged to use them personally while working with clients. They may be used at any point during a session, whenever centering, relaxing, grounding, or receptivity might be helpful.

Breathing awareness and muscle relaxation

Breathing awareness

Of the general methods for relaxing attention, breathing awareness is perhaps the most important. Probably nothing affects consciousness more than breathing. Simply stated, no breath, no life. The precious gift of life is born or "inspired" anew with each inhalation, and dies or "expires" again with each exhalation. In stress we lose awareness of our breath. It becomes constricted and irregular, and we are thus unable to process experience (i.e., to let life "move through"). Our consciousness is no longer breath-based and breath-created, but muscle-based and restrictive. Muscle-constricted thinking is profoundly conservative: it dams the river of life flowing through the somatic self, leaving one isolated in the fixed understandings and frames of the cognitive self. Thus, the same patterns of "doing and viewing" will occur. This is especially troubling in areas of symptomatic behavior, where the old ways of responding have predictably unsatisfying outcomes. Thus, a major tool in changing behavior is returning consciousness to a breath-based awareness.

Many practices are helpful in the regard. One simple meditation technique is counting the in-breath and out-breath. The therapist may do this for himself and/or suggest it to the client; both may benefit. The first step is to develop a comfortable, relaxed sitting position with the back straight and hands uncrossed. A few deep breaths may be taken to release tension in the muscles. The eyes may focus gently on the tip of the nose or on a point on the ground about five feet in front of you. (Alternatively, attention may gently rest in the awareness of the abdominal muscle that rises and falls with each breath.) Rather than breathing in, let the breath come in. (One metaphor is God breathing air into Adam's nostrils in the myth of creation.) As the breath comes in through the nostrils, filling up the lower diaphragm, say silently, "breathing in, one." As the breath goes out, say silently, "breathing out, one." For the next breath, the inhalation is marked with "breathing in, two," the exhalation with "breathing out, two," and so on with each breath.

When practicing this skill, you may experience many distractions. Each time you notice that you've lost your place, just gently come back, either beginning anew or continuing where you left off. Let each breath dissipate the mental images and thoughts locked into your awareness. The point is to experience awareness without control or analysis, with a growing experience of freshness, suppleness, and solidness.

Training breath awareness seems so simple, yet it is quite a challenge and remarkably helpful in alleviating unwanted thinking and behaving. The basic idea is that to be possessed or gripped by negative sponsors, a person must first shut down the breath of life. Since this is such a chronic and hence unconscious activity, we are seldom aware of when we do it and its negative effects. By beginning to notice the correlation between breathing and quality of experience, a person may pursue the benefits of training breathing awareness. The goal is to let each experience and thought keep moving through awareness, so identification is released.

One simple therapeutic application of this practice is to ask about an antagonistic image, thought, or feeling: do you sense it "inside" or "outside" your breath? Usually, difficult processes are experienced outside the breath. When you concentrate on breath and then experiment with gently bringing the troubling image, thought, or feeling inside the breath, a significant shift in relationship to this "antagonistic other" often occurs. We will expand on this idea in the discussion of the Tibetan practice of tonglen in the next chapter.

Muscle relaxation

Chapter 1 introduced the principle that the river of life moves through you, except when it doesn't. The idea was that as experience flows through a person, the unwillingness or inability to "be with" a given experience leads to a neuromuscular lock—a fight or flight response—that blocks processing of that experience and shuts down receptivity to new experience. When chronically held, neuromuscular lock becomes habituated—that is, a person is tense and blocked without even being consciously aware of it—and unprocessed experiences remain in a sort "purgatorial" no-man's land in the somatic self (see Shapiro, 1995; van der Kolk, 1994). *This is the "neglected self" in self-relations.* Thus, a crucial skill of the therapist is detecting and loosening muscular locking in the course of therapeutic conversation. In addition to breathing awareness, there are other approaches helpful in muscular relaxation, including relaxed concentration, weight on the underside, and softening agitation.

1. *Relaxed concentration.* Following the Errol Flynn principle noted in Chapter 2, the interest in self-relations is in developing the "not too tight, not too loose" experience of relaxation. The point is not to be passive, groggy, or tranced out, but fresh, solid, and free in feeling and responsiveness. This might be done by relaxing into areas of tension, rather than trying to "get rid of" the tension.

A classic method for doing this is the progressive relaxation method in which a person is instructed to tense and then relax each successive area of the body. For example, the person may be asked to focus on the feet, tense all the muscles there, and then let go of the tension as breath is released. The same process is repeated for the ankles, the calves, and so on up to the top of the head. The therapist may also apply this procedure with himself at any point during the session in order to be more receptive and grounded.

The same method may be used in a less methodical way. The person may be asked to scan the body, allowing attention to tune into any areas of significant tension, and then apply the "focus and relax" process. For example, a client complained that she developed intense tension in her belly whenever she talked with her boyfriend. He was encouraging her to "lighten up" and let go, to just get into the flow of things. Her belly felt more and more tense. I suggested she listen and attend even more to the feeling in her belly, but to do so without too much muscular tension. This was a bit difficult at first, but as she continued this "concentrate and relax" process, she felt more centered and attentive to herself and to her boyfriend. She was able to assert herself in a centered, direct way, and felt both stronger and more tender with herself in the process. The point was not to abandon her "gut feeling," but, rather, to develop the skill of focusing even more but with less tension. This skill of deep concentration without muscular contraction is a chief characteristic of hypnosis and meditation, as well as a hallmark of a skillful, mature consciousness. It reflects the capacity to use mental process without disconnecting from nature, so that both worlds—description and experience—may work cooperatively.

The target may also be an external focus. For example, the therapist might use this technique discreetly while talking with clients. He might focus attention on the client, then relax all around the focus while maintaining the concentration. This can be repeated until a sense of relaxed concentration is developed.[1] This state is generally characterized by expanded awareness of the relational field that holds observer and observed, as well as reduced analytical chatter. There is a felt sense of groundedness while sensations and images "flow through" awareness. It is especially helpful for the therapist when the client's presentation is difficult to track or otherwise distracting. It is akin to what a dancer does with a partner, or what a basketball player or martial artist does with an opponent: develop a soft but concentrated focus that reduces reactivity to the "fakes" while enhancing connectedness to the person's center. In therapeutic terms, it allows the therapist to stay in tune with the client, regardless of where the client's story line leads. The client may move off into mental fantasy, but the therapist remains grounded with a "felt sense" of the neglected self. This helps the therapist gently return attention to the reality of the present moment.

In self-relations, this process of sliding into mental fantasies is

---

[1] The experience and value of concentrated relaxation that includes an external focus has been emphasized by the psychiatrist Arthur Deikman (1963, 1966). In talking about his concept of "deautomized experience," wherein a person sheds the "shell of automatic perception, of automatic affective and cognitive controls in order to perceive more deeply into reality" (in Tart, 1969, p. 222), Deikman emphasized that this state was developed by intense external focus along with letting go of the usual modes of analytical thinking and perceiving.

Similarly, the experience of "flow" has been extensively researched and discussed by the psychologist Mihaly Csikszentmihalyi (1990). In the experience of flow, intense focus and relaxation are both critical. Thinking becomes clearer and sharper, even as the person develops what Gendlin (1978) calls a "felt sense" of this experience.

called "touch and go." It means that when the therapeutic conversation touches the tender soft spot of the client, the client often automatically moves attention—both his own and the therapist's—away from this vulnerable place of the neglected self. For example, the client may suddenly shift topics. If the therapist's attention is not stable in a good relaxed concentration, he may be distracted and lose track of the critical event in the therapy, namely, the return into awareness of the neglected self.

2. *Weight on the underside.* Another way to relax muscle tension is to encourage attention to the "underside" of each muscle group—the bottoms of the feet, the backs of the legs and arms, the bottom of the ears, etc. (Tohei, 1976). The idea is to experience gravity gently calming you down, allowing a feeling of grounding and centering to develop.

A related technique is to attend to the sensations in the curved areas of the body—for example, the gentle curves of the wrist, the curved space from the inside of the thumb up the side of the index finger, the curve of the neck sloping down the shoulder, or the inside of the elbow. This simple attentiveness brings awareness to the body in a gentle way, reducing internal chatter and increasing responsiveness to the present moment.

3. *Soften agitation.* In the common state of neuromuscular lock, most of our experience, thinking, and acting arises from an underlying state of agitation (fear, anger, or desire). A simple exercise to help decrease agitation is to move through a series of gentle self-suggestions for "soft mind . . . soft body . . . soft eyes . . . soft heart . . . soft soul." (Additional suggestions for tense areas such as the jaw, forehead, and shoulders may be included.) The idea is simply to bring mindfulness to each area, so that muscular holding may be released.

For example, in softening the mind, it may help to adopt the Buddhist view that mind is space and that space is sky. The field in which the thoughts move is felt as "full emptiness" or "openness." The idea or suggestion of "soft mind" is given, along with an invitation for a receptive response. It may help to feel the most dense area, the busiest "downtown" area of the mind—for most people, this is in the head—and start there. With training it is possible to develop a mindfulness that is full of a direct, felt sense of awareness without trying to fix things. Again, this can be helpful to both therapists and clients. The goal is not a sloppy or reduced mental presence, but an increased clarity without the agitation.

If the mind is agitated, it's very hard to relax the body, and vice versa. So it's good to cycle through the different areas. The point, which is central to many martial arts, is that true resilience, strength, and courage come from softening the agitation. This is different from the prevailing notion that "harder is better." We favor "hard-headed" ideas over "soft-headed" ones, scowl at somebody for being too soft, and demand that we "buckle down" and get to work. Given this bias, it's no wonder we may take "soft-mind" to mean becoming mushy headed or spacey. On the contrary, it means better concentration, better responsiveness, and better perceptual acuity. In any performance art, relaxed alertness is crucial. This state requires a soft flexibility that is the basis for precise execution and flexibility. It is this complementary state of gentle precision that we are interested in developing with the methods of this chapter.

Centering attention

Of five Jewish thinkers who made good, the first was Moses, who pointed to the head and exclaimed, "Focus on the commandments, on logos. If you concentrate on keeping those in your head, you can't go wrong." Next came Jesus, who pointed to the heart and emphasized that if you concentrate your attention there, all good things would happen. Third, Karl Marx arrived on the scene, touching the solar plexus while talking about brotherhood and courage. Freud, of course, pointed lower in theorizing about the important centers of consciousness. Finally, Albert Einstein came along and put in all in perspective when he observed, "It's all relative."

—*Anonymous joke*

When a person is feeling stuck or isolated, attention is often concentrated in the head or projected away from the body. One simple principle to restore balance is to center and drop attention lower into the body, its different centers of consciousness, and the earth supporting the body. This principle is central to all martial arts (as well as other performance arts). It is also reflected in the general hypnotic suggestion to "drop down" and "go deeper" into trance, as well as the soulful idiomatic encouragement to "get down."

Heart centering

Thinking from the heart is just as important as thinking from the head. As Pascal commented, the heart has its reasons that reason knows nothing about. (It is interesting to note that heart disease is the number 1 disease in America.) We might say that language (and the mind) is powerful, evocative, and creative when it synchronizes with the beat of the heart. Certainly in hypnosis or poetry we look to coordinate these two orders of being. The basic idea is that when mental process is linked to the biological drum beat in the body, mind-nature coordination is achieved and the creative potential is activated. Just as important, entrainment of awareness with heartbeat brings calmness and grounding. The mental chatter diminishes and a "heart-felt" centering develops.

One simple four-step heart-centering process is as follows. The first step involves relaxing and opening up. This may be done by sitting comfortably, taking a few deep breaths, letting attentiveness move to the breath, and letting go of control.

In the second step, one feels the physical presence of the heartbeat. This may take a little time, and it may help to gently touch the heart area with one or two fingers to focus attention. The goal is to just tune into the felt sense of the heartbeat, perhaps noting any changes that begin to occur (e.g., calming down, decreased chatter).

In the third step, one senses a second heartbeat inside the first heartbeat. This may take a bit of gentle patience and listening to experience. A person might use any of a variety of names for this second presence—spirit, the inner self, the unconscious—or use no name at all. The point is to notice the centering and opening of awareness that occur when you feel a second heartbeat.

The final step involves the repeated use of a word, phrase, or sentence. This could be thought of as a prayer, a mantra, an affirmation, a hypnotic suggestion, or whatever else makes sense to a person. For example, Table 4.1 lists nine prayers suggested by the Vietnamese Buddhist monk Thich Nhat Hanh. In using a list such as this, a person may select out the one(s) that feels most helpful or relevant. The idea is then to use the statement to open the heart as a place for experiential centering and thinking.

Of course, other words, phrases, or sentences may also be used. Possible words include "openness," "tenderness," "safety," "acceptance," and "centering." Phrases might include "it's going to be okay," "this too shall pass," "let it go," and so forth.

Each of the four steps—relaxing and opening, listening to the

---

TABLE 4.1. THE NINE PRAYERS[2]

1. May I be peaceful, happy, and light in body and spirit.
2. May I be free from injury. May I live in safety.
3. May I be free from disturbance, fear, anxiety, and worry.
4. May I learn to look at myself with the eyes of understanding and love.
5. May I be able to recognize and touch the seeds of joy and happiness in my life.
6. May I learn to identify and see the sources of anger, craving, and delusion in myself.
7. May I know how to nourish the seeds of joy in myself every day.
8. May I be able to live fresh, solid, and free.
9. May I be free from attachment and aversion, but not be indifferent.

---

[2] Reprinted from *The Mindfulness Bell: Newsletter of the Order of Interbeing,* (Issue no. 15, Winter 1995–96, Community of Mindful Living, P. O. Box 7355 Berkeley, CA 94707). As Thich Nhat Hanh adds: "After practicing 'May I be . . . ,' you can practice 'May he (or she) be . . . ,' visualizing first someone you like, then the one you love the most, then someone who is neutral to you, and finally the person whom thinking of makes you suffer the most. Then you can practice, 'May they be . . . ,' beginning with the group, the people, the nation, or the species you like, then the one you love, then the one that is neutral to you, and finally the one you suffer the most when you think of."

heart beat, feeling the second beat, adding a prayer or affirmation—is dependent upon the previous one(s). For example, comfortably feeling the heart beat will be very difficult without some sort of softening in the body. So if any step becomes difficult, a person may simply return to an earlier step before proceeding.

Disconnection from the heart center is implicated in various difficulties. Self observation will reveal that when a problem comes up, the heart center shuts down. Control strategies predominate as receptive and intuitive facilities recede. The feelings in the heart area are another form of the fressen energy of the natural self. If the cognitive self does not sponsor it, it will feel like an antagonistic symptom (fear or pain) that has no human value and should be avoided or numbed. By bringing attentiveness back to what's happening in the heart center, a person may practice mindfulness to allow it to reveal its human value and helpful nature.

One way to do this is by asking the question, "What do I need to be at peace with right now?" (The therapist may ask this of himself during a session, or ask the client to answer it for himself.) The question is not intended to be answered so much intellectually as with a felt sense. For example, the person might notice that as he thinks of his job, an angry tense feeling is in his heart. By using the four-step heart centering method, the person may explore thinking about his job *while* softening and opening his heart; in fact, he may bring the thoughts within the space of the heart. Painful feelings in the heart may be frightening, partly because of a general belief that we cannot bear to have heart to be "broken." So we often move away from these feelings, shutting down around them and withdrawing our sponsorship. If we can appreciate that such feelings indicate an opening of the heart to a deeper core tenderness, sponsorship may return and positive experiences can occur. We begin to develop a "rational heart," a discerning place of tender sobriety where a person can stay in the reality of the moment without shutting down.

Listening from the heart does not mean abandoning the analytical processes of the head. It means integrating thinking with feeling. It especially means bringing mental process back into (its) nature, like a singer singing with the music rather than in front of it. Chapter 6 examines in depth how this may be used to resolve

problematic experiences. For now, the emphasis is simply on noticing that multiple centers of consciousness exist in the somatic
self and that both therapist and client may be helped by tuning
into them.

Belly centering

Centering in the heart may not always be the best place. For
example, in dealing with anger or fear it may be more helpful to
drop attention lower into the belly, several inches below the navel. Many Eastern traditions assume the mind is located in the
belly: as D. T. Suzuki (1960) points out, the primary purpose of
the koan method in Zen Buddhism is to shift attention from the
mind in the head to the mind in the belly. Also, martial arts
strongly emphasize that both perception and responsiveness origi-
nate and should be centered in the belly.

Recent research in the West has provided fascinating scientific
confirmation of this idea. The new field of neurogastroenterology
is based on discoveries of a complex and hidden brain in the gut
that is able to learn, act, remember, and "think" independently
from the brain proper (Blakeslee, 1996). The enteric nervous system, as it is called, is thought to be an earlier brain developed
when we were tubular animals sticking to rocks and waiting for
food to come by. (Many of us can still remember this era of the
Sixties!) M. D. Gershon (see Gershon, Kirchgessner, & Wade,
1994) has reported that the enteric nervous system contains a
complex network of neurons, neurotransmitters, and proteins
that operates autonomously from the brain proper. It produces
"gut feelings" that, if attended to, may inform and guide a person's activities. If unattended to, they may take the form of ul-
cers, "angry bowel" syndrome, or chronic fear.

I vividly remember an experience with my daughter Zoe regarding the "belly mind." When she had just turned four I took
her and a couple of her friends to the beach. The girls were
climbing four- to five-foot high cliffs and jumping off into the
sand. As Zoe moved to higher ground, she excitedly called to
everybody to "watch this really high jump." Asking me to count
and build up the drama, she poised on the cliff. Just as she was
about to jump, her eyes fluttered as she looked down and touched

her belly, saying, "Oh, my tummy's scared!" I suggested she move to a lower launching point, but she insisted upon her present place. The situation repeated itself three or four times before she graciously accepted a few assurances and some simple coaching tips (on breathing and focusing the eyes outward) in order to successfully help her jump. Since that time, we talk often about what her "tummy" is telling her.

The vital idea in self-relations, emanating from Milton Erickson's legacy, is that listening to and "being with" an experiential response allows its human value to emerge. *Love is a transformative act that requires great courage and skill.* Rather than repressing, dissociating, or becoming identified with belly feelings, we can connect with them in a way that shifts our whole relational experience of them and ourselves. The belly center offers a "place" to hold experience so that it may be sponsored and transformed. In the next chapter, we will see how this may be done via the Tibetan practice of tonglen.

Vertical relatedness: Connecting multiple centers

Other bodymind centers may be distinguished. In Hindu traditions, there are seven "chakra" centers, including the crown of the head, the "third eye," the throat, the heart, the solar plexus, the point right below the navel, and the root chakra (in the perineum). Whether or not one subscribes to these notions, they suggest a way to reunite mind and body relationships and dissolve the tyranny and isolation of the disconnected cognitive self.

One simple exercise is called "chakra cleaning." The person assumes a relaxed, open posture and then starts with, say, the heart chakra. Orienting attention to the heart, the person imagines a jewel in its center, noting its color, shape, type, etc. Further attention is paid to any accumulated dirt or other obstructions to the radiance of the jewel. The person then imagines gently cleaning the jewel, sensing the gradual increase in its shine and beauty. This same process is then repeated with another chakra center. Each time a "jewel" is cleansed, the person may connect it to the already shining jewels, building a progressive string of radiant jewels, each with its own characteristics, all bound by an energetic link. This type of exercise may promote deeper relaxation, greater openness, and more bodymind connectedness. It may be elaborated and modified in a variety of ways.

A clinical application of centering

Centering is helpful in many ways. In stressful situations individuals often "give themselves away" to an outside source. By reclaiming one's center, one may reclaim oneself and move from reactivity to creative responsiveness. To sense where the self is projected, one may ask the question, "*To what (or whom) do you give first attention?*" First attention may be thought of like the cursor on a computer screen; it can be moved around wherever you want. For example, say a couple is fighting with each other. One points her finger and raises her voice. In reaction, the other's eyes fix in fear or anger on the partner, his body tense and rigid. Each partner gives "first attention" to the other, projecting it through the eyes and fixating it on the partner, who is then experienced as "causing" one's behavior and experience. This is what is meant by giving oneself away.

The alternative is to return first attention to one's center. The person might take a deep breath, open attention to the relational field, drop attention into his belly, and respond from a felt sense of his center. *This is a learned skill, not an automatic response.* It involves the rigorous training of an alternative to the "fight or flight" response wherein one loses one's center; this third way is called "flow" in aikido.

This loss of centering may also be seen when a client accesses an emotional experience. As his eyes well momentarily with tears, his arms may cross over his stomach as he looks up and away at the ceiling. (This is another example of the "touch and go" process.) Through his eyes he projects himself (imaginally) out of his body and onto the wall. (By watching a person's eyes we can often see where first attention is given.) With his cognitive self projected away from the body (which is a common strategy for trauma survivors), the person is uncentered and feels overwhelmed and "exposed" in the experience. *The "stressor" becomes the influential other or "higher power" that determines identity.* In other words, when one moves first attention away from his center, he is open to living under the influence of alienation or other forms of negative sponsorship. *The antidote for alienation is returning to one's center.* A person always has "first dibs" on his tender soft spot; it is only by leaving his center that alien sponsors may take over. As Nathan Sharansky (1988) emphasized as his main principle during years of imprisonment as a Soviet dissident, "nobody can humiliate me except me."

Centering practices provide an opportunity to realize this extraordinary principle of living from one's center. In aikido, part of this training involves developing "soft eyes" and dropping awareness to a center point a few inches below the navel. It may help to let your fingers touch that point in your body and rest gently until harmonization with breathing is felt. This may take a while and require some gentle coaching, so patience and tenderness are especially helpful.

The therapist can learn to drop into the "belly-mind" when stressed and can help clients learn to do so as well. The basic idea is that, when "first attention" is given to your center, you will be more receptive and respond more effectively to both yourself and others. Being receptive doesn't mean you allow a person to run you over. As an exercise in martial arts, connecting with your center is about increasing the freedom to feel secure and to respond nonviolently from a deep sense of love.[3]

The underlying premise here is that your relation to your center (or what some might call their soul, or sobriety, or daemon) is your primary commitment. It is more important than any other relationship in your life—your kids, your mate, your work—since without it you cannot remain present. This idea of the primacy of self-love is new for many, so it is important to distinguish narcissistic absorption from responsible self-love. In narcissism, you move away from the world and into your mental projections; in centering into self-love, you are more fully in the reality of each moment, connected to both self and the world around you. The simple notion, testable in action, is that when

---

[3] Gandhi used to say that if the only alternative to passive submission to injustice was violent resistance, he would recommend violent resistance in virtually every case, since none deserved unjust treatment. But he emphasized the third possibility of *satyagraha,* which we translated earlier as "firmness of soul" or "force of love." Gandhi emphasized how this nonviolent force could be effectively used to meet and transform the force of violence. Aikido uses this same principle, as does self-relations work. All require the skillfulness of centering practices as their basis for realizing this extraordinary principle.

you leave your center you cannot sustain being with anything or anyone else. You make a mess of things, whatever your intention. Centering allows you to let life move through you and thus to allow awareness to include, but also extend beyond, the narrow interests of the cognitive self.

Grounding

In martial arts, as in other performance arts (such as dancing), attentiveness is also given to the support of the ground. The idea is that in stress a person's energy is not rooted solidly in the ground and he can thus be imbalanced and "pushed around" easily. Conversely, feeling a connection with the earth allows a supple sense of solidness and presence.

The principle of grounding may be helpful for people dealing with stressful situations. Usually, at such times attention is either on oneself or on the other. Attention may be exclusively in cognitive processes and not on the somatic centering and the (literal) common ground shared by the persons involved. Grounding practices may reconnect the person with the somatic self and allow a greater responsiveness and flexibility. Grounding may be especially helpful for the therapist, who must be able to be listen to a number of painful stories while remaining open and responsive.

One way to ground is simply to soften the eyes, take a breath, and allow awareness to "drop" into the ground. A feeling of spaciousness may be developed, along with a sense of being supported by an infinitely curved earth. Thus, rather than feeling toe to toe or head to head with a person in a narrow field, one may feel a great open space where the relationship may occur. This is not a dreamy altered state, but an enhanced state of relaxed alertness, where the space between the therapist and client is softened and opened. It may help to feel one's belly center press gently down into the earth, perhaps feeling it extend all the way to the core of the earth. It may also help to feel a gentle energy pressing down through the balls of the feet, while simultaneously feeling an energy coming up from the earth through the heels of the feet. Again, these are basic exercises taken from martial arts that are designed to help one feel fresh, solid, and free to respond creatively. They may also have value in other relational performances such as psychotherapy.

Opening attention

The complementary principle to dropping attention into one's center is opening attention to the relational field. This is based on the simple observation that in symptomatic behavior attention generally constricts, often fixating rigidly on the figure of the stressor, withdrawn from the field around it. An aikido principle relevant in this regard is: *Never fix your focus on the attack.* As Morihei Ueshiba (in Stephens, 1992), the founder of aikido, wrote:

Do not stare into the eyes of your opponent:
he may mesmerize you.
Do not fix your gaze on his sword:
he may intimidate you.
Do not focus your gaze on your opponent at all:
he may absorb your energy.
The essence of training is to bring your
opponent into your sphere.
Then you can stand where you like.

Below we explore four techniques for opening the field.

Evenly suspended attention

Opening attention is very similar to Freud's idea of "evenly suspended attention," which he described as crucial to the therapist's state of consciousness:

Suspend . . . judgment and give . . . impartial attention to everything there is to observe." (Freud, 1909, p. 23)

(The technique) . . . is a very simple one. . . . As we shall see, it rejects the use of any special expedient (even that of taking notes). It consists simply in not directing one's notice to anything in particular and in maintaining the same "evenly suspended attention" (as I have called it) in the face of all that one hears.

. . . For as soon as anyone deliberately concentrates his attention to a certain degree, he begins to select from the material before him; one point will be fixed in his mind with particular clearness and some other will be correspondingly disregarded, and in making this selection he will be following his expectation or inclination. This, however, is precisely what must not be done. In making the selection, if he follows his expectations he is in danger of never finding anything but what he already knows; and if he follows inclinations he will certainly falsify what he may perceive. It must not be forgotten that the things one hears are for the most part things whose meaning is only recognized later. (Freud, 1912, pp. 111–112)

This evenly suspended attention is developed by softening attention and letting it spread through the relational field. This is similar to the advice Don Juan gave to Carlos Castenada (1974) in *Tales of Power*, when he recommended that Carlos learn to walk with eyes spread to 180 degrees peripheral vision, watching the horizon on both sides while feeling his hands at his sides. (Don Juan added the further sobering suggestion to then sense death always stalking you over your left shoulder!) We might call this *field-based* perception, rather than the more traditional figure-based perception. It is a sort of "juggler's consciousness" that allows one to connect with the relational field holding different figures (truths, people, positions, etc.), without locking into any of them.

Three-point attention

One simple way to achieve a field-based attention is through what I call three-point attention. I sometimes introduce this to clients as an "anti-anxiety" technique, pointing out that, in order to worry, you have to tense your eyes and then move them around in arrhythmic patterns. (This is why in a traditional hypnotic induction a person is asked to relax and focus on a point: it disrupts the orienting response triggered by eye movements and thereby sets hypnosis into action. I also believe it is a major reason for the success of EMDR therapy, which asks clients to rhythmically entrain their eye movements to the therapist's finger movements while processing traumatic memories.) I then suggest a simple experiment, namely that the client relax and allow a first point of attention to develop in his belly (or heart, or hands, whichever is most comfortable). I then suggest that he select two other external points to focus on, preferably one on either side of me. We work a bit on relaxation and on gently distributing attention until all three points are equally in focus. I then suggest the client soften the attentional field a bit more while remaining alert. Thus, the person develops a equi-point spreading of attention in the field, with a soft focus and grounded sense.

A nice aspect of this technique is that the therapist can easily monitor how the person is doing. If the eyes shift, gentle coaching suggestions to relax and refocus can be given. This is a straightforward way to develop a relaxed and alert focus. (Again, the therapist can do this in parallel with the person.) Therapy work, especially with anxiety-related issues, can then be done with the client in this state. It keeps a person from accessing control/fear reactions to an experience, thereby allowing him to stay present.

The client may be encouraged to develop this process before or during stressful situations as a centering method. It is also helpful when a person is having trouble getting to sleep. Usually, a person has his eyes closed and is tossing and turning in bed. In using three-point attention, it is suggested that the person lay on his back with his arms at his side. Eyes are to be kept open, with a person trying not to blink. Three-point attention is established while looking toward the ceiling. (In a darkened room, the points are projected in space with the eyes open.) The person will find the eyes wanting to roam all over the place, but gentle refocusing will allow the three-point field to relax the somatic self and bring relaxation and sleep to the person.

Relational entrainment of attention

A modification of this exercise is what might be called "relational mind" circuits. This is a quasi-hypnotic experiential process that is designed to entrain attention with another person. I have used it with couples, as a training exercise for therapists, and occasionally with clients. I use it unobtrusively at times to deepen a sense of connection with the client during an interview.

To develop this entrainment, a person develops the feeling of gentle pulsating bands of energy that move through him and his partner, connecting them in elliptical orbits. For example, a person first senses a gentle energy behind his eyes, a relaxing feeling that can be felt as a pulsating band of energy frequencies. This curved band can extend through the temples of the forehead into an orbital circuit, moving through the temples and behind the eyes of his partner. Similar orbital loops may be developed through the ears, the fingertips, and toes. The partners allow their attention to rest within the field, noting what awarenesses are being sent and received through these relational loops.

This process may sound strange, but it is a simple way to feel an intimate "pattern that connects" you and another person. It encourages an experience of mind as a relational field between people rather than a static position inside a person's head. The idea is that the more you can move from the isolation of being locked inside your head to the relational field that connects you with others, the less life is sensed as a problem.

Remembering experiences of self-transcendence

We noted earlier that virtually all people have had unitive experiences of communion wherein they experience a connection to something beyond their individual selves. These experiences may develop through simple practices such as playing with children, knitting, swimming, reading, praying, engaging in athletics or art, or walking on the beach. As we noted, such experiences of self-transcendence reveal an presence greater than our cognitive selves. Asking a person to recall and revivify such experiences is another way to open attention. As we discussed in Chapter 3, a person may access the relational field as a context for working with difficult experiences.

Cleansing the doors of perception

A final set of practices has do with washing away the "dust of everyday living" that obscures clarity.

Erasing hypnotic phenomena

All of this talk about softness and relaxation is bound to result in some people drifting off into trance, so it should be reiterated that this is usually not the goal in following these principles. In fact, a major goal is to help people awaken from low-grade states of trance-like attention. A few common side effects of hypnosis are grogginess, distortion of reality, and diminished behavioral responsiveness. Since these may detract from therapeutic presence as well as effective responsiveness in challenging situations, it is helpful to have a few ways to steer away from them. That is, an important skill is the capacity to expand into the relational field without slipping into trance. A simple question may be asked in this regard: *how do you know you are going into trance?*

The most common answer is trance phenomena. That is, one knows trance is developing because the phenomena (or appearances) of subjective experience change significantly. These changes may occur in visual, somatic, auditory, or cognitive representational systems. They can sometimes have a narcotic-like effect that distorts experience and takes a person further away from being present in the moment. This may be helpful and interesting in some situations—for example, for mental exploration or interior work—but distracting and unhelpful in other situations—for example, a therapist needing to tune in to the client, or a person wanting to stay connected in a relationship.

So it is useful to have the choice to develop or erase hypnotic phenomena. To accomplish the latter, here is a simple experiment. Find a comfortable position and take a few moments to get into a receptive state. Tuning to your visual awareness, ask, "What is the first (small) sign that trance is developing?" It could be a tunnel vision, or a certain type of imagery, or a shift in detail. As you notice whatever it is, take an imaginary "gentle, mental eraser" and tenderly erase that phenomenon. Then feel what's behind it (not in the sense of a hidden meaning or symbol, but the experiential space—often openness—that is sensed). As you feel what's behind it, let yourself move deeper into a "trance" (without the trance phenomenon).

Next move your attention to your body and ask the same question: "What is the first small sign that trance is developing?" It could be a heaviness in the body, a tingling in the hands, or a dissociative feeling. Take the gentle, mental eraser and erase that distortion. Feel what's behind that, and go deeper into trance as a result. Repeat the same for the cognitive realm, and then recycle through each modality as many times as you'd like.

This exercise can help a person experience a place that is neither the dictatorial control of ego identity nor the dreaminess of hypnotic reality. It can help develop an exquisite awareness of the middle way between the extremes. Here life is not a problem: it simply "is." This can help one deal more directly with life on life's terms.

Erasing cognitive phenomena

On the one extreme we lose ourselves to the seductiveness of fantasy and image, on the other to the thought-forms and constructs of the cognitive self. We become addicted to thinking, rigidly applying rehearsed mental structures. We believe that we think thoughts rather than, as Nietzche emphasized, thoughts thinking us.

When thinking becomes unhelpful—that is, a person feels stuck, overloaded, tense—the same "experiments in consciousness" used with hypnotic phenomena can be applied to analytical content. Thus, after the person has centered, opened attention, softened the mind/body/heart, etc., and erased the hypnotic phenomena, he may wonder, "What else am I aware of?" As each thought, image, or percept is noted, the "gentle mental eraser" may soften or fully erase it, allowing a felt sense of the open tender space behind it. The place from which a person is observing the thoughts may also be felt and gently and tenderly erased. This allows another type of experience of mind as a relational field. Like Milton Erickson's "middle of nowhere" or Deepak Chopra's (1989) "field of all possibilities," it is a space from which fresh experience can arise. It provides relief from compulsive doing/thinking and a return to the more basic experience of mindfulness. This is an antidote for the mind caught in the endless cycle of performance. An experience of peace and curiosity may develop, and a renewal of self-love may be found.

Summary

Lasting or recurrent problems usually reflect a break in relatedness between the somatic self and the cognitive self, with the resulting loss of both one's center and a connection to the larger relational field. The way attention is used is especially prominent in maintaining such states. At the heart of each symptom is a general agitation or neuromuscular lock that is blocking the life force and its resources.[4] Thus, it is important to develop skills that identify and relieve neuromuscular lock, allowing the reunion of mind and nature, thinking and feeling. The general methods that we have explored here—breathing and muscular relaxation, dropping and centering attention, opening attention, and cleansing the doors of perception—are a few suggestions for how this process might be accomplished. As it occurs, mindfulness and relatedness are again possible, thereby potentiating healing and growth.

[4] This idea of a general underlying factor of agitation or disturbance in all psychological symptoms is reminiscent of Hans Selye's (1956) proposal of the stress factor. Selye described how when he was a young doctor examining patients in a hospital, he was struck how they all looked sick—that is, regardless of the diagnosis, they all seemed to share some general look of illness. This led him to propose that stress was an underlying factor in all illness. The ideas of neuromuscular lock and agitation are used in a similar way in self-relations.

5

LOVE AS A SKILL

THE PRACTICES OF SPONSORSHIP

Psychoanalysis is in essence a cure through love.

—Sigmund Freud, in a letter to Carl Jung

Love is the productive form of relatedness to others and to oneself. It implies responsibility, care, respect, and knowledge, and the wish for the other person to grow and develop. It is the expression of intimacy between two human beings under the condition of the preservation of each other's integrity.

—Erich Fromm, 1947, p. 51

A BASIC PREMISE of self-relations is that the river of life courses through each of us, bringing every experience known to humankind. In this sense, life is out to get us, helping us to become more and more of a human being. Life cannot be fooled: we cannot avoid the basic experiences of fear, joy, anger, sadness, excitement, envy, and so forth. The basic question is our relationship to this river of life. We can fear and try to damn it, ignore and exploit it, or accept and work with it. It is this latter relational skill that we call love.

In examining love as a courage and a skill, self-relations emphasizes the principle and practices of sponsorship, whereby the agency of mindfulness may touch and "be with" something as a means to bring human value and transformation to it. The corollary of this is that whatever is unchanging in human experience is not being sponsored. Thus, the skills of sponsorship allow the natural process of change to occur. Sponsorship occurs in many different contexts: a parent with a child, a person with her own experiences, a therapist with a client, an artist with archetypal or artistic processes, a friend with a person in need, a person in nature. In each situation, the fressen energies of life are flowing, and sponsorship is the skill by which such energies are cultivated into the vital essen forms of human being. As we will see in this chapter, sponsorship skills include deep listening, proper naming, providing a place, expressing, blessing, connecting, disciplining, protecting, encouraging, and challenging.

In applying these ideas of sponsorship to psychotherapy, we are guided by three interlocking principles: (1) join and sponsor the presenting self; (2) access the complementary self; and (3) develop a relational self that connects the two selves. To see how these principles are practiced, we first explore an exercise in naming and integrating complementary selves. From there we examine some basic therapy skills of sponsorship. Finally, a modified version of the Tibetan practice of tonglen ("giving and receiving"), a remarkable method for transforming negative experience, is discussed.

A prototype exercise: Who are you?

This is a straightforward way to introduce the three interrelated principles of joining, complementing, and connecting in psychotherapy training groups. Figure 5.1 shows the by now familiar diagram of joining complementary selves into a relational self. To do this in the exercise, groups of three are formed. One person is in the client position; a second is Therapist A; the third is Therapist B. (Roles are rotated, so everybody gets a chance at each role.) Everybody first takes a few minutes to settle in and relax. (The attentional practices of Chapter 4 are helpful in this regard.)

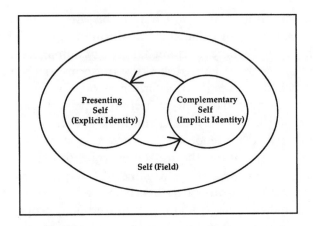

FIGURE 5.1. SELF IDENTITY AS RELATIONAL OPPOSITES

Step 1: Joining with the presenting identity

When ready, Therapist A orients to the client, nonverbally connects with open curiosity, then asks, "Who are you?" The client allows the question to filter through the somatic self, like a hypnotic suggestion or a poem, noting any responses that arise. (Clients are generally asked beforehand to limit responses to social identities they have experienced in their personal history: I am a sad three-year-old boy, I am my father's son, I am a therapist, I am Zoe's father, I am a husband, I am a reader of books, etc.) Whatever the response, the client speaks it as a simple statement, for example, "I am my father's son."

Therapist A receives this statement and lets it touch and reverberate through her somatic self. The intent is not intellectual understanding but experiential seeing of who the client is, for example, as his father's son. The identity may be sensed by the therapist in terms of its energetic resonance as well other nonverbal elements such as posture, tone, intensity, etc. This is crucial: both client and therapists are primarily looking for a felt sense of the identity. The identity of "my father's son," for example, is meaningless simply at a cognitive level. If we lined up five "father's sons," we would have five very different emotional and psychological "ego states." So the therapist feels through the verbal description to sense the person's experiential state connected to the description. *It is the experiential state of the somatic self that the therapist looks to tune to and be with.*

As Therapist A receives the identity, she is interested in "holding it," that is, giving it a place in the centers of her somatic self. This is one of the most crucial skills of the self-relations therapist. It is similar to how a person might be open to music, to a poem or any other art form, or to loving a child, especially when the child is in stress. As the therapist feels the identity spoken by the client, she also feels how to be with it, how to vibrationally connect with it, how to fit with it. This takes at least a few moments of silence, allowing the intelligence of the somatic self to receive and hold an identity. The therapist might bring the identity into her heart center or her belly center. Once this is done, Therapist A simply says, "Yes, I see that you are (your father's son)."[1]

Step 2: Accessing a complementary identity

Meanwhile, back at the ranch, Therapist B has been silently participating, receiving and holding the identity spoken by the client. As Therapist A acknowledges the spoken identity, Therapist B lets it go and feels for an opposite or complementary identity. For example, a complementary identity to "father's son" might be "mother's son" or "daughter's father" or "your own person." There are many possible complements. To sense one, the therapist does not proceed primarily on an intellectual or semantic basis, but rather on an intuitive one. As the first identity is taken in and held within a somatic center, the question of feeling an opposite energy or way of being elicits a complementary felt sense, along with a verbal description. Thus, when Therapist B senses the complementary identity, she tunes into it and speaks to it by saying, "And I also see that you are (your daughter's father)."

The point is not to scientifically name, but to poetically evoke and complement. The complement may fit well, or only partially, or not at all. Any response is useful, as long as the therapist remains sensitive to the client's response.

---

[1] This "seeing" is more than the sensing of a perceptual object, for example, "I see the ball on the floor." It is the existential "seeing" of sponsorship that includes a blessing. That is, the person's beingness is sensed, touched, and honored in the process.

Step 3: Experiencing both identities simultaneously

After Therapist B makes her statement, the therapists pause and then say simultaneously, "And what a nice thing to know that you can enjoy BOTH at the same time!"[2] Again, the stereophonic delivery is poetic and hypnotic, as well as playful, encouraging the client to feel the presence of both identities simultaneously.

To reiterate, the simultaneous activation of different truths, ego states, or identities in the nervous system is a succinct formula for developing an altered state of consciousness. The person "loses her mind" for a moment as points of views create an interference pattern (like a hologram), and what's typically left is a feeling of integration, openness, and delight. (This, of course, assumes a supportive context; in a nonsupportive or violent context, the resultant altered state is painful and unintegrated, since there is no unitive field present.) Identity moves from a position-based cognition (I am this or I am that) to a field-based knowing (I am the relational field that holds descriptions). This provides a glimpse of the generative consciousness of the relational self.

After a few moments of allowing the response to develop, Therapist B takes the lead by asking with curiosity, "And who else are you?" This precipitates another round of the three steps of eliciting and acknowledging an identity, intuiting and accessing a complementary identity, and stereophonically activating a field that connects both identities. Usually about four or five rounds are done, each one deepening the involvement. Then partners rotate roles and repeat the exercise.

The exercise can be done with just one therapist. (Indeed, using it in therapy usually involves a single therapist.) The point is that the therapist looks to connect with and acknowledge whatever identity/social role/ego state the person presents (e.g., I am a problem, I am a trauma survivor). He next feels for and

---

[2] Some have questioned the word "enjoy" in the statement. Partly the exercise is done with an Irish twinkle or its equivalent, such that enjoyment is a key theme. Partly it is done to emphasize the possibility of a positive relational feeling toward a negative experiential response. Thus, when I recall an old incident, I needn't be bound by the feeling of that incident. The important quality is self-love or self-connection during such recalls. Of course, other words such as "experience" may be substituted for "enjoy."

speaks to a complementary identity in the person's experience (e.g., I am resourceful, I am competent), and then works to connect the two into a relational self. In clinical practice, the timing will vary tremendously. The therapist may need to take much longer—up to several sessions—to be with the presenting (problem) identity before its felt sense is acknowledged and held relationally. Also, the client may slip out of the resource state long before it gets integrated. The process is not so different from working with couples, where the truths of each person must be validated and held against each other to allow for a deeper truth of the relational self to emerge. Thus, it takes skill to apply the principles embodied in the exercise in clinical practice.

This exercise is especially helpful when a client is stuck in a neglected self. For example, a professional woman in her forties described a series of relationships with men where she had initially become close and then critical and distant. Her father had been an abusive alcoholic who abandoned the family when she was an adolescent. The first part of the therapy concentrated on acknowledging her right to choose, to say no, to feel and respect her boundaries, and to voice her interests. This seemed to open the possibility for a greater intimacy, which in turned seemed to arouse paralyzing fears.

I did the exercise with her. Each time she voiced a fear—for example, "I am afraid that I will be abandoned again"—I would receive it, hold it, and feed it back: "I see that you are someone who is afraid of abandonment." After pausing to let it sink in, I would acknowledge the complement: "And I also see that you are someone who has learned to enjoy her independence." After pausing to let that sink in, I would acknowledge both: "And what a nice thing to know you can enjoy both *at the same time.*" This would usually create a intense feeling of something shifting deep within her somatic self. I would then ask: "And what else are you afraid of?" and a new cycle of integrating complementary identities would begin. After five or six cycles, a feeling of deep calm and tender openness developed, wherein she felt both vulnerable and strong. We gently talked about how this feeling was different from how it was when she was an adolescent and how she could use this new context to make room for her fears as well as her resources.

Figure 5.1 reminds us that every explicit position presented by the client is connected to an implicit position. Therapy is a conversation that draws relational awareness within and between these circles, so that each truth or position has a place, with none in isolation. When the self is relational, the spirit of life is once again felt.

The figure also reminds us that we can start in any of the three places: joining and acknowledging the explicit or dominant position (e.g., the problem-defined self), or speaking directly to an implicit position (e.g., a competent or resource-based self), or speaking first to the creation of a field without reference to the positions.

When the therapy is stuck, the principles suggest three possible causes. The first is that a present identity state has not been fully sponsored. Usually this means a neglected self is dominant. Perhaps it has not even been noticed; or perhaps it has not been properly named, felt, or valued. Given the fears and other anxieties connected to the neglected self ("If I let myself feel this, something terrible will happen"), this is the rule rather than the exception. The "touch and go" strategies, wherein a person touches the tender soft spot of her experiences and then goes away someplace else, are typically operative. Thus, joining, remain connected with, and further sponsoring a neglected self often take considerable patience and skill. The most important first step is for the therapist to "do nothing": let go, relax, center, open, soften, clear out, and let the neglected self come into your awareness.

Second, the client may not feel capable of staying in relationship with the neglected self. In that case, the therapist might direct attention to a competency-based cognitive self. For example, solution-oriented therapy does this by inquiring about "exceptions," or times when the problem is not occurring (de Shazer, 1985). Narrative therapy does it by asking about times when the client successfully "resisted" the alienating ideas that induce the problem-saturated state (White & Epston, 1990). As we will see in the next chapter, self-relations asks questions such as, "What are the things you like to do best?" and "When do you feel most like yourself?"

Third, a relational field may not be felt, making it difficult to hold differences or allow transformation to occur. Thus, the therapist might introduce a meditation or hypnotic process to open the field. Any of the techniques described in the last chapter are helpful in this regard.

Skills of sponsorship

The source of love is deep in us, and we can help others realize a lot of happiness. One word, one action, or one thought can reduce another person's suffering and bring him joy. One word can give comfort and confidence, destroy doubt, help someone avoid a mistake, reconcile a conflict, or open the door to liberation. One action can save a person's life or help him take advantage of a rare opportunity. One thought can do the same, because thoughts always lead to words and actions. If love is in our heart, every thought, word, and deed can bring about a miracle. Because understanding is the very foundation of love, words and actions that emerge from our love are always helpful.

—*Thich Nhat Hanh, 1991, p. 78*

Successful use of the "complementary self" exercise and its variants requires proper timing, rhythm, and nonverbal resonance. Lacking a hypnotic or poetic base to activate the somatic self, the exercise is superficial, uninteresting psychobabble. But when the words of the cognitive self arise from and remain connected with the somatic self, the results can be quite powerful. The underlying idea is that when clients present with a problem, they describe an impotence where what they say or do makes no difference to how they feel or would like to be in certain situations. Self-relations says that in part this reflects a disconnection of speaking and thinking from the nonverbal centers of consciousness. We therefore seek to reconnect what is being said with what is being experienced. As Varela, Thompson, and Rosch (1993) have lucidly noted, this connection of the domains of description and experience is a crucial aspect of any postmodern, humanistic science.

The exercise suggests a number of sponsorship skills involved in fostering this reconnection process. Table 5.1 lists thirteen that are especially used in the self-relations approach.

TABLE 5.1. SKILLS OF THERAPEUTIC SPONSORSHIP

1. Connecting with self
2. Connecting with the other
3. Curiosity
4. Receptivity
5. Touching and holding an experiential truth
6. Proper naming
7. Letting go
8. Noticing exceptions, differences, and other complementary truths
9. Identifying and challenging self-negating influences
10. Sensing the relational field that holds the different identities
11. Holding multiple truths simultaneously
12. Speaking to multiple truths simultaneously
13. Knowing when and how to push the reset button

---

1. Connecting with self

We saw in the last chapter how this process includes centering, grounding, and opening within and beyond oneself. In the absence of such a connection, a model tends to be applied ideologically and thus oppressively. Thus, *the most important commitment a sponsor has is to herself*. Without a connection to herself, a person will tend to be reactive rather than responsive, engaged in fight (domination) or flight (submission) patterns rather than true relational engagement. Through cultivating self-love, a person discovers a deeper trust and acceptance of both interior and exterior life. The fressen energies of life flow through the therapist's consciousness, providing an entirely different type of guidance than the cognitive self can give. Thus, the self-relations therapist is committed to an ongoing connection with herself throughout a session. Whenever it is lost, getting it back (e.g., via exercises of Chapter 4) becomes a priority.

2. Connecting with the other

Nonverbal connectedness with the client is equally important and involves similar methods. Relational practices include deep listening, silence, and a receptive mode. Too often therapy, like most of contemporary life, relies primarily on an active mode, such that the primary question of both client and therapist is "What do we do?" In order to effectively do, we need to practice not-doing and not-knowing (Erickson & Rossi, 1979). In the present context, that means opening a receptive mode so that experience can "come find you." To develop this type of attention, one follows the Errol Flynn principle of "not too tight, not too loose."

The important thing is to experience a felt sense of the client's somatic self. For example, the therapist might relax into her breathing in order to feel the client's breathing against her own. She might soften her eyes to sense the client's emotional patterns as movements in a field, with a texture and a color. (This is the way some musicians perceive music, and it may be the way some therapists sense emotional patterns.) Attention might be widened to sense the relational field that allows whatever the client is doing or experiencing to have a place. All these sorts of relational connections require a relational self that joins the somatic self with the cognitive self while sensing the field from which both arise. When awareness is connected with a center, a relationship of self and other(s), and the relational field, mature and effective love is possible.

3. Curiosity

Once relationally connected, the therapist may become curious about various identity-related questions, such as: Who are you? You're up to something big—what is it? Something is awakening within you; what is it? These questions are usually held silently by the therapist as she connects with the client. The intent is to concentrate on holding the question (not too tight, not too loose), letting the answers come.

These general questions held internally by the therapist will lead to specific questions asked of the client: What's going on? What's the problem? How is it a problem? What do you think you need to get rid of? Where in your body do you most feel the center of the problem? When asking such questions, it is especially important that the therapist notes both the client's answers and her own. Too often the client is held solely responsible for answering the therapist's questions. In a relational approach, both the therapist's and the client's responses are equally important. Thus, if the therapist asks, "What do you need?", she notices both the client's and her own responses to the question. The holding of these two responses together is what allows therapeutic conversation to occur, especially when there are differences between the responses. For example, the client may say she needs to try harder, whereas the therapist notes an incredible weariness and a need for rest. *In a relational approach, both answers are equally valid.* When they are held simultaneously, interesting developments occur. Indeed, it is precisely the reconnection of the client's responses with other perspectives (i.e., conversation) that allows creative possibilities to emerge.

4. Receptivity

The skill of holding a question leads to the skill of receiving an answer. The important thing is to maintain a disciplined listening, gentle but precise. Often nothing will come at first; then from the silence arise feelings, images, words, and other symbols. If the therapist does not cultivate the patience and confidence to sit in silence, this process cannot occur. If the client asks the therapist why she is silent, the therapist may simply, honestly respond that she is curious about a question and waiting for a response. This may lead to a discussion about how the client may benefit from a similar practice of self-listening.

Here we want to be touched deeply by the client's experience, especially the fressen energies coming through her somatic self. R. D. Laing (1987) warned against therapist "psychophobia," where therapists are terrified of the client's psychological processes. We are afraid that if we open up to our clients' experience, we will be infected or overwhelmed by whatever is ailing them. Yet a basic principle of healing is that it is possible to accept and transform painful experiences. To reiterate Merton (1964), tyranny and oppression develop when we believe negative experiences cannot be transformed. We turn away from them in fear and then return to them with anger, malice, and violence. So for healing purposes, we must finds ways to open and be with each aspect of the client's experience.

To do this, therapists must avoid being sentimental and over-identified or disconnected and separate. A middle way is possible, wherein experience is allowed to "proceed through" the nervous systems of both therapist and client. This is the "life flowing through" premise of self-relations, where the principles of mindfulness and sponsorship transform fressen energy into essen forms.

Willingness to open to the client's suffering is important in another way. A major misunderstanding underlying suffering is that the pain a person is experiencing is merely personal. That is, a person believes the sadness she feels is because of things that happened or didn't happen, or that the fear she feels is because she lacks courage. Yet these feelings are inevitable parts of life: If you are alive, fear will visit you. If you are alive, anger will visit you. If you are alive, sadness will visit you. There is no escape from it, though there are ways through it. But if we believe that it is only an expression of our personal condition and not also a universal aspect of the human condition, we will isolate and otherwise break our relatedness to the rest of the world.

When the therapist opens to the client's pain, she recognizes and accepts it as a human condition that she also shares. This "sharing of suffering" is, of course, the experience of compassion. It moves the experience from something separating and stigmatizing to something connecting and humanizing. Both the therapist and client will feel a greater freedom and openness in finding helpful ways to be in relationship with the shared experience. This doesn't exclude the fact that the meanings and details of the experience are personal and hence unique for each person; rather, it expands beyond it to include a communal context that allows the personal to be changed.

5. Touching and holding an experiential truth

As the therapist attends to the client's fressen energies, she will notice that the client is unable or unwilling to hold, acknowledge, or otherwise be with certain experiences involving fear, anger, desire, or other feelings. These unsponsored experiences constitute the neglected self of the client. Since unsponsored experiences (1) seem to have no human value and (2) will repeat themselves until sponsored, a major focus of therapy is how to bring sponsorship to them. One aspect of sponsorship is providing a place for human life to exist and develop. For emotional feelings, this means a place in the bodymind of the somatic self. The therapist can help by opening a center in her somatic self to touch and hold the client's neglected self.

For example, say a client describes a problem with her husband. She talks about feeling angry and then exploding into rage or withdrawing into silence. The problem is not her anger: again, anger is an inevitable part of the river of life flowing through each of us. The problem is that when the anger comes, she goes away. It acts out without her human presence to hold it and guide its expression. So the solution is to help her feel and hold the anger in ways that allow it become a part of the solution.

The therapist might begin by asking the client where in her body she feels the emotional experience is centered. (Again, the therapist might note her own intuitive response to this and check it against the answer given by the client.) Say the client points to her belly. The therapist opens that same center within herself and invites the experience of anger to rest within it while simultaneously asking the client to do the same within her own center. The therapist might encourage the client (and herself) to touch the anger with breathing, and silently talk with it, as if talking with a child or a friend. Perhaps two fingers might touch the area of the body to maintain attention in that center.

To reiterate, the problem is that when the client experiences the problem her attention is destabilized and the neglected self has no "place" or "home." The feeling will then project out of the body (e.g., onto another person) or splinter into pieces or be pressed down. If a center can be cultivated for the feeling, it can be listened to, calmed, and cultivated into a resource. *To help this process, the therapist allows herself to be touched by the client's neglected self.* Feel where in your bodymind it touches you, and then open a center to gently but firmly provide a place for it. As the client moves from the experience, keep it within your center. This will help you bring the client's attention back to her center and gradually sponsor and integrate the out-of-control experience.

In thinking of the somatic centers as "places" to hold emotional experiences, one must distinguish the feeling center from the emotional experience held in that center. Thus, I can bring an uncomfortable feeling of sadness into the secure and comfortable feeling of a somatic center, in much the same way a calm and loving parent may bring a scared child into her arms. This is what Virginia Satir meant when she used to ask two questions of a person: "How do you feel about that?" and "How do you feel about feeling that?" The first question refers to the emotional experience, the second to the somatic center in which it is held. The second feeling is a context that determines the meaning of and responsiveness to the first feeling, so it tends to be more important for therapy concerns.

As an experience is given place, it will tend to change. This is a characteristic of what Merton (1948) called effective suffering. Thus, an anxious client may initially describe an experience as a knot in her chest. As she begins to sponsor it, it may change into the experience of a frightened eight-year-old girl. With further attentiveness, it may change into a curious and happy eight-year-old girl, then an image of a field of flowers, then a wise old woman, and so on. The point is that the somatic self has no fixed identity; through it flows all the archetypal experiences.

6. Proper naming

As the Biblical myth reminds us, in the beginning was the word. Until an experience is properly named, it does not exist in human being. (And as the existentialists say, until a person is blessed and "seen" by another, she does not exist.) We have emphasized how proper naming is not scientific classification or detached labeling. Proper naming involves seeing an experience, touching it with human presence, holding it, and giving it blessing. Without this implicit ethical base of love and respect, the named experience will have no human value.

We can see the importance of proper naming with children. They initially do not know how to name basic experiences such as hunger, fatigue, anger, and loneliness. When such states and their attendant demands occur, they respond with pure fressen energy: crying, crankiness, whining, and so forth. (This is precisely the same unsponsored energy that characterizes adult clients in symptomatic states. As Erickson said, neurosis is the inability to speak directly.) Caregivers have to note and read these cues in a child, asking themselves, "What state (hunger, fatigue) needs to be attended to?" Kids learn to name and hence recognize and attend to these states as they mature. But if neglect occurs or a certain state is rejected or otherwise cursed, the proper naming may never occur. The states still come, but they have no human sponsorship. In such cases the fressen energy of the state may overwhelm the person, as can be seen in any symptomatic state. The experience seems to have no value to self or others, and thus defensive or violent measures are taken against it.

It is interesting in this regard to note that a major acronym used in Alcoholics Anonymous is HALT, which standings for hungry–angry–lonely–tired. The idea is that if these states are not properly named and recognized when they occur—and they occur regularly for each of us—the person is more susceptible to self-medicating through drugs and alcohol. *Drugs, alcohol, and other destructive agents serve as false sponsors for the neglected self.* The same could be said for any problematic state—its recurrence is likely when a feeling goes unnamed and unrecognized.

We can sense an experience that has not been properly named— that is, a neglected self—whenever a client withdraws, distracts, acts out, or otherwise relationally disconnects. Therapists may also recognize the onset of a neglected self by monitoring their own somatic selves, noting when in the therapy conversation they begin to experience agitation, unpleasant feelings, stuckness, spacing out, or sleepiness. Another sign is that the therapeutic conversation is circling around the same pattern over and over, with nothing changing. For example, the client may be complaining about a relationship, but each time the therapist attempts to directly address it, the topic changes or attention is otherwise redirected.

In such circumstances, something is happening that is not immediately apparent. In self-relations terms, a neglected self is active in the somatic self but not sponsored by the cognitive self. *This is the norm, not the exception, in therapy conversations; it is precisely why the client is talking with the therapist.* The challenge is how to name the problem that has no name, and then bring human blessing and sponsorship to it. The very fact that it has no name means that the cognitive self should not lead the search; rather, the therapist should allow the neglected self to find and touch her somatic self first. This is akin to the "evenly suspended attention" state described in the last chapter—the therapist centers, opens attention, develops receptivity and curiosity, and thereby enters into a relational field with the client.

Once connected to the relational field (which holds both therapist and client), the therapist may contemplate the identity question of "What experience is not being acknowledged?" (This is usually done silently, although the therapist may sometimes ask the question aloud.) As responses come, the therapist may "be with" them in a grounded and open way. They might then be shared directly with the client; for example, the therapist might say, "As I listen to you, I sense the presence of fear." If this seems too threatening to the person, it may be helpful to start with acknowledging a complementary competent self ("I sense the presence of a very committed, courageous person") or use less direct methods such as story-telling (see Gilligan, 1987).

When a neglected self is properly named, calmness typically results. The somatic self has been touched, and feeling and experiential absorption deepen. The client's eyes might moisten and a relational connection with the therapist intensifies. This may last only seconds, before the person moves away from the neglected self once again. (This is the "touch and go" pattern, wherein the tender soft spot is touched and then person has to abandon it). The important thing is for the therapist to remain centered, open, and alert. *As the client abandons her neglected self, the therapist stays with it.* She holds it in her somatic self and wonders how to gently return attention to it. The experience of the neglected self might be immediately addressed, or a complementary competent self might first be accessed to provide resources.

7. Letting go

A complementary skill to touching and holding an identity is releasing it in one's attention. Since self-relations is primarily concerned with the relational connection between differences, it's important to know each perspective, but not identify solely with any given one. It is like listening to a complex symphony, where attention opens to one piece, then another, then the whole. Similarly, the therapist is interested in being with one client identity, then another, then the field that contains both. This requires knowing how and when to let go of being with a given identity.

This is especially obvious when working with couples. The therapist listens to one partner, validating and giving blessing to a particular experience, e.g., fear of abandonment. She must then gently release that experience, orient to the other partner, and sense which neglected self needs to be named and sponsored. Attention may then move to identifying intensely angry or attacking parts of each person, as well as loving and nurturing parts. If the goal is to find ways to relationally connect these different selves—both interpersonally and intrapersonally—the skill of releasing each one to open to another is important. You gotta know when to hold them, and when to fold them.

The same, of course, can be said when working with an individual. One of the problems with problems is their self-locking properties: once a person gets into a state, she has a hard time getting out of it. Learning how to let go is thus important to both therapist and clients. The "not too tight, not too loose" attentional skills explored in Chapter 4 are helpful in this regard.

8. Noticing exceptions, differences, and other complementary truths

In traditional psychotherapy, attention usually organizes around the problem identity of the client. Recent correctives to that tradition have included Ericksonian psychotherapy, solution-oriented work, and narrative therapy (see Gilligan & Price, 1993). The basic idea is that problems persist when a person gets locked into a neglected self, and that solutions emerge when communications access other identities that include a person's competencies and resources.

A great example of this may be found in Milton Erickson's case of the African Violet Queen of Milwaukee (reported in Zeig, 1980). A wealthy, single 52-year-old woman lived alone in her big house in Milwaukee. She was horribly isolated and depressed, venturing out only to attend church services on a daily basis. Her depression worsened to the point that her nephew, a physician who was in therapy with Erickson, feared she would commit suicide. He asked Erickson to visit the woman during an upcoming trip he was making to Milwaukee, hoping he might be able somehow to help her.

Erickson arranged to meet the woman in her home. From talking with her and touring her home, he noted three different identities. First, she was indeed depressed and isolated, with a passive response style. Second, she was deeply religious and committed to her church (even though she never talked to anyone). And third, she grew some beautiful African violet plants in her sunroom.

The first identity is what we might call the problem-based, dominant identity. Traditional therapy would primarily understand and communicate with the person around this identity. But Erickson noticed the second two identities—what she was doing when she was not depressed (or who she was in addition to being depressed). He then became curious about how new patterns might emerge via those complementary identities. He got the woman to raise more African violets. He then asked her to notice each time a person or family in the church community was going through some important transitional event—a birth, death, marriage, graduation, retirement, etc.—and to give that person or family an African violet to honor the event.

The woman became too busy to be depressed. And people began to notice and appreciate her, going out of their way to talk with her. She became quite active and loved in the community. When she died some twenty years later, hundreds came to her funeral to mourn the passing of the African Violet Queen of Milwaukee.

The principle here is clear. Problems arise when a single identity is isolated from the family of identities. Solutions occur when relatedness between multiple identities is brought into play. The therapist is thus always curious about who the client is in addition to the presenting identity.

This orientation to complementary truths may be helped by a simple verbal technique originally suggested to me by Bill O'Hanlon. For every description of reality, the respondent simply says (with conviction), "That's always true," and then adds the caveat, ". . . except when it's not." (An Irish twinkle or its equivalent is helpful in the delivery.) Thus, the client might say, "I'm a terrible person," and the therapist might simply add, either in her head or aloud, "except when you're not." Or, "this theory is true . . . except when it's not"; "my wife doesn't understand me . . . except when she does"; "this client is resistant . . . except when she isn't." Inserted into the conversation, this verbal response is a humorous yet serious way to loosen the dehabilitating spell of fundamentalism that posits exclusive truth. It can acknowledge a truth while opening to its complements.

My colleague Tully Ruderman came up with an interesting elaboration of this technique. Person A says, "I'm always this way . . . except when I'm not." She then orients to her partner and adds, "you're always this way," which Person B receives and adds, "except when I'm not." Person B then says, "I'm always (another way) . . . except when I'm not . . . you're always (this other way)," which Person A completes with "except when I'm not," and so on. For example:

Person A: I'm always critical (*pause to let it sink in*) except when I'm not (*pause to let it sink in*). You're always critical . . .
Person B: except when I'm not (*pause*). I'm always right (*pause*) except when I'm not. . . . You're always right . . .
A: except when I'm not. . . . I'm always needy . . . except when I'm not. . . . You're always needy . . .
B: except when I'm not (*and so on*).

This exercise may done with couples or with therapist and client. It is a fascinating process that leads to a mutual recognition that each person holds complementary identities. It can liberate persons from fixed positions and limiting understandings of self and other.

9. Identifying and challenging self-negating processes

A person may come under the spell of damaging influences—curses, drugs and alcohol, violence, or self-defeating processes. A good sponsor is able to skillfully identify, protect, challenge, and build immunity from such processes. In self-relations, the two major "negative sponsors" are "aliens" and "self-intoxicating inductions." As we have seen, alienating ideas include "you're unlovable," "you'll always mess up," and "you're stupid." If unchecked, they act like what Robert Dilts (personal communication) calls "thought viruses" that infiltrate and damage an entire system.

Closely related to the idea of aliens are self-intoxicating inductions such as self-pity, depression, grandiosity, whining, and jealousy. The idea is that when a person experiences a primary feeling—sadness, fear, love, anger—she may numb it or "drug it" with these negative inductions. This will produce what the Buddhists call the "near enemy" of an experience. A "near enemy" looks like an experience, but is actually its opposite. Sentimentality is the near enemy of love, and self-pity the near enemy of compassion. Self-intoxicating inductions are "overlays" on a feeling that makes it toxic and impossible to swallow. A good sponsor will thus recognize and depotentiate such negative inductions. As we will see, this is a delicate operation requiring skill and relational trust, since the negative induction is deeply intertwined with the experience of pain.

The next chapter examines in greater detail how the therapist may work with negative sponsors. For now, a brief example may help. A client who grew up in abusive home had many years of therapy. He would typically begin to complain about being alone and unloved. As he did, he sounded "whiny" and looked self-absorbed. Taking a few minutes to center myself, I listened and then said in a gentle but serious voice, "You're whining." He looked startled and continued in his same vein. I paused and repeated, "You're whining." He looked bewildered, trying to read my intent.

"You don't care about me," he shot back.

"Sure I care about you," I responded, ". . . but you're whining."

He looked distressed. "Well, I want to have things different in my life. I'm just trying to tell you how I feel."

"I understand. You're feeling bad. You want things to be different. And you're whining." I smiled slightly and so did he.

"Well, what the hell else can I do?"

"Well, you can talk about your experience without whining."

This led to a discussion of how to experience and communicate without whining. The nonverbal way in which such a conversation is conducted is obviously crucial. If the therapist sounds critical or judging, it won't be helpful. The therapist needs to appreciate that it's okay if the client whines, but it probably isn't helping the client achieve her goals. This may be pointed out in a straightforward way.

In challenging clients in this way, it may be helpful to sense how self-intoxicating strategies are ways, albeit ineffective, by which the cognitive self tries to protect the tender soft spot of the somatic self from further damage. Thus, while the therapist can sense the genuine pain coming from the somatic self, she must also sense how that pain is being perpetuated by outdated defense strategies. By skillfully challenging such strategies, the therapy may "pop the bubble" of suffering that engulfs a person. Chapter 6 further explores how this might be done.

10. Sensing the relational field that holds the different identities

As multiple identities become apparent, it is crucial to sense the relational field to which they all belong and in which they have a place. In the absence of this felt sense, the relational self that draws connections between these differences is difficult to realize. This field may be felt within the body, within the relational space of the therapist and client, or within a larger field. The techniques of opening attention described in the last chapter can be helpful in this regard.

11. Holding multiple truths simultaneously

Each ego state or identity of a person is like a state-dependent complex, with its own physical, psychological, and behavioral values. This means that usually only one identity is active at a time, which makes relational connections among identities difficult. By learning to hold several simultaneously, one is freed from overidentification with any single position. *This is the essence of the relational self.* One way to do this is by holding different identities in different centers of consciousness.

LOVE AS A SKILL

This is an especially helpful skill in parenting, where one is faced with the dual challenges to (1) love your child unconditionally and (2) help her become a social citizen. (The God that created these contradictory demands surely has a perverse sense of humor.) To effectively discipline rather than punish a child, a parent needs to feel love for her even when emphasizing that her behavior needs to change. (It is important that in this principle we strive for progress, not perfection.) One way to do this is by cultivating a felt sense of "she's a great kid" in one bodymind center (e.g., the heart) while holding another felt sense of "she needs to change her behavior" in another bodymind center (e.g., the gut). With practice, this relational connection can improve parenting skills.

A similar process may be practiced with oneself or with a client. If a fear is felt, one can hold it in one bodymind center while holding a mindful and accepting presence in another center. It is the skill of holding both at the same time that allows growth and emotional learning to occur. The next chapter explains this method in greater detail.

12. Speaking to multiple truths simultaneously

Having activated different identities, the therapist faces the next sponsorship task of facilitating relational connections between them. This is like doing therapy with couples: we remain curious about how each perspective complements the other until we see how each perspective contributes to a bigger, more complete picture. While doing this, it is important to stay connected with somatic rhythms.

For example, Don was 35-year-old single man. His therapy goal was to meet women and become more socially active. He described a very abusive childhood where his father assaulted him regularly. His presenting persona was pretty tense and loud, with a soft and shy underside to it. He described how he would go to singles events with a determination to approach attractive women and introduce himself in a "confident and powerful way." To his dismay, he would usually flip from this rather overbearing mode into a submissive, self-denigrating state, sometimes before even saying a word. Self-criticism, withdrawal, and humiliation would follow, and he would slink away to make renewed vows to "overcome" his fears once and for all.

This description suggested two selves, one aggressive and the other fearful. *The lack of relational connection between them makes each of them unhelpful.* Thus, the self-relations therapist seeks to facilitate this relational conversation. I read Don Robert Bly's poem, "Four ways of knowledge," which includes the following passage:

> What to do . . . to stall her.
> To fight or to flee—
> He didn't know. He wanted
> to fight *and* to flee. (1986, p. 164)

We identified where in his body he felt the fear, and where he felt the aggressiveness. With some coaching and conversation, Don learned how to sense both at the same time so that each experience tempered the other, creating a third feeling of an integral self that was tenderly focused and stayed connected within himself as he extended to others.

13. Knowing when and how to push the reset button

It is important to know when to stop using these sponsorship skills. One obvious point is when a process is completed. Another is when, for whatever reason, the client (or the therapist) cannot process any further at a given time. A rest may be needed. A third common reason to stop is that what's happening is not helpful. Somehow, perceptions are off, relational connections are not strong, or the point is being missed. At such times, it's wise to desist from "doing" and regain "being with" one's center. This skill of realizing that what one is doing is not helpful is crucial. Relaxing and pushing the "reset button" allows a fresh, receptive orientation to occur, enabling new understandings and applications of the principle of sponsorship.

The techniques of sponsorship we have touched upon here are just a few possibilities. You will find many other ways that are helpful to you and your clients. The important understanding is that we can bring our human presence to touch and help transform suffering into growth and self-acceptance.

A modified practice of tonglen

The river of life that moves through each of us brings every experience known to humankind, and then some. If you are alive, you will repeatedly experience happiness, sadness, fear, interest, anger, pleasure, and so forth. This is not a function of circumstance, but of life itself. The key variable is what you do with these natural fressen energies surging through you. Self-relations suggests that via sponsorship one can use these basic everyday experiences to develop personhood.

The practice of sponsorship may be applied in many ways. An example is the ancient Tibetan practice of *tonglen,* which means "sending and receiving." Chogyam Trungpa (1993) and his student Pema Chodron (1994) have described this method as central to Tibetan approaches to working with "negative" emotional experiences involving anger, sadness, fear, or other suffering. They emphasize that while you cannot avoid such experiences, you can skillfully use them as the basis for developing self-love and love for the world. The method is somewhat counterintuitive to the consumerist Western mind, which is trained to want to take in all the good experiences and dump out all the "bad" experiences. In tonglen, the negative experiences are taken in, and positive experiences are given away to the world. In this way, one practices the skill of transmuting suffering into grace.

In thinking of suffering, it may be helpful to recall Thomas Merton's (1948) comment that he did not become a monk to suffer more than other people, but rather to suffer more effectively. Effective suffering is suffering that results in deeper confidence, more self-love and love for others, and greater responsiveness and flexibility. This is quite different from the self-flagellating suffering that many are taught in formal religions.

There are a number of ways that the tonglen method may be practiced. Table 5.2 shows a modified method helpful for therapy purposes. First, a target experience is identified—some person, experience, emotion, or part of oneself that a person wants to

TABLE 5.2. FOUR STEPS IN MODIFIED TONGLEN PROCESS

1. Identify "negative" target experience
2. Identify self-transcendent experience
3. Develop breathing connection to relational self
4. Circular process: Breathe in target experience/Breathe out self-transcendent experience

change. This can be easily identified by filling in the blank: *If only I didn't experience X, there wouldn't be a problem*, where X is a toxic experience, behavior, or person in one's life. For example, it might be a client's depressive behavior or dependency needs, a spouse's indifference, or one's own perceived laziness or fear. A person may use a 1–10 rating scale, where 1 is "not very intense" and 10 is "very intense," to select an appropriate target (low enough to be manageable, high enough to be meaningful). At first, this may be a low intensity item; as one gains confidence in the tonglen method, higher intensity items may be used.

Along with identifying a negative item, the person finds a positive memory or relationship with a person, place, or process that involves the experience of love and openness. It is easy for me, for example, to do this by thinking of my daughter. Other examples might be a memory of a sunset or vacation, a beloved friend, or a time of deep self-love. It is an experience that lets you know the extraordinary beauty and love that exists in the world.

To reiterate, most Western traditions try to hold onto the "positive" experience and get rid of the "negative" experience. In tonglen, sometimes referred to as "exchanging self for other," the relationship is reversed. The negative experience is breathed into one's center, to be touched with kindness and transmuted with mindfulness, while the positive experience is breathed out into the world, to help create a world to which all belong.

In order to do this, it is crucial to first develop a state of centering, grounding, and openness. Without a stable attention, tonglen could be a painful and unhelpful experience. One should also cultivate an awareness of the belly center of consciousness, where breath may be drawn. Mindful breathing is cultivated and maintained to allow the experiences to ride the breath in and out, not getting stuck anywhere.

Once a person is centered and open, the toxic experience may be sensed. On the inbreath, it rides the breath into one's center, where it is gently received and touched with kindness and mindfulness. On the outbreath, the positive experience is sent into the world. On the inbreath, the negative experience again rides into one's center; on the outbreath, the positive experience surfs into the environment. This steady gentle rhythm may be reiterated for as long as seems appropriate—five minutes, ten minutes, or longer. (In monastic practice, it is sometimes recommended as an around-the-clock exercise.) The person is just noting any differences or changes in the understanding, perception, or experience of either the positive or the negative.

The usual effect is the detoxifying of the "negative" experience, as well as a deeper understanding of its true nature. For example, say a client is complaining about her childhood. This has been going on for a number of sessions, and attempts to work with it or shift the conversational focus have failed miserably. The client keeps going on and on, and the therapist notes herself feeling exhausted, distracted, angry, and uncentered. This suggests that a neglected self is active and unsponsored (in both client and therapist). The therapist might proceed by first letting go of trying to help or change things—indeed, sometimes trying to be a therapist is the least therapeutic act one can engage in. She might concentrate instead on centering, breathing, grounding, and opening attention. She might sense the feeling of stuckness in the client and, when ready, start the tonglen process of breathing in the neglected self and breathing out love and acceptance. As she does, the sense of the neglected self will often become clearer. Perhaps she will sense an unnamed young child who is full of hope and excitement as well as fear and anger. Continuing the tonglen, the sponsorship of the neglected self may develop to include a deep love and understanding of these experiences within the client. Talking with the client from this centered and accepting place may then lead some helpful directions, as we will see in Chapters 6–8.

This type of practice is connected to a number of venerable traditions. It is, of course, the basis of the Christian ethic of transforming sin via love. It was the basis of Gandhi's principle of *satyagraha*. The transmutation of negative experiences is not done through mere "positive thinking" or sweet feeling. It is an act of courage and skill. Witness the lives of Christ, Martin Luther King, Victor Frankl, Gandhi, Nathan Sharansky, Nelson Mandela, and many other courageous individuals. They point to the possibility and power of love. The value of their work is in suggesting that we may learn to do the same, each in our own way. While the challenge seems great, what are the alternatives?

The principle and practices of transforming negative experiences are also the basis of the martial art of aikido. In Japanese, "ai" has two meanings: "reconciliation of conflict" and "love." "Ki" ("chi" in Chinese, or "holy spirit" in Christian circles) is the universal life force that moves through everything. "Do" (as in aikido, judo, Tae Kwon Do) is "the Way" or "path." So aikido means "the way of reconciling violence by joining with the universal life force of love." In practice, one deals with violent attacks by first drawing them into one's belly center.

The same principle is at the heart of Milton Erickson's legacy (see Rossi, 1980a, b, c, d). Erickson emphasized that therapy involved the acceptance of whatever the client brought in, no matter how crazy, unuseful, or negative it might seem. His utilization approach involved joining with such behaviors and experiences with the curiosity and commitment to discover how they might become the basis for change and self-discovery. In short, Erickson's approach was based on the courage to love.

At a practical level, we are faced with similar challenges on a daily basis. We can start by observing our fear and agitation as they arise around certain experiences in our clients. We can examine our own resistance and cynicism to the idea that nonviolence is a powerful force of healing. We can note our own conditioned responses that accept violence and oppression as justified. We can try little experiments of cultivating an open heart and acceptance of negative experience, in order to find ways to exercise sponsorship and mindfulness as our basic relational processes.

A central idea in all of this is that the safest place to be with a challenging or antagonistic experience is in one's center. In the eye of the storm, all is calm. We are often taught that we can get contaminated or infected by the client's process if we open our hearts to it. Tonglen and its cousin practices are traditions and methods by which a therapist may overcome her fear of the client's experiences and use her skills to help transform the difficult ones. Thus, tonglen is a major example of the practice of sponsorship that is central to self-relations psychotherapy.

There are many ways in which the practice may be applied. The therapist may be doing it from the beginning of a session, opening the breath to receive into one's center whatever difficult experiences are being identified by the client, letting the positive experiences flow on the outbreath. In this way, the therapist neither dissociates nor identifies with the problems of the clients, but finds ways to bring them into the moment-to-moment mindfulness of the conversation, where new relationships and possibilities may emerge.

At any point in the session, it may be introduced more formally to the client. This can be done in different ways. The next chapter describes the prototype method of self-relations therapy, where painful experiences are separated from alienating influences and reconnected with resources.

Summary

If you are alive, the river of life will course through, bringing on a daily basis a multitude of experiences. You will be touched by every emotion known to humankind: happiness, sadness, anger, excitement, disgust, and so on. If you think life is out to get you, you're right; the basic question is what it wants from you. Self-relations assumes that life wants you to grow and develop as a human being. Thus, each experience it brings you is part of the growth process. The crucial skill—indeed, the greatest gift of humanness—is the capacity to skillfully love what is given to you.

The principle and practices of sponsorship are central in this regard. Sponsorship is the relational process by which we connect with, touch, bless, guide, provide place and proper constraints, introduce traditions, and otherwise support a living presence to assume human value. Without sponsorship, an experience will have no name, no voice, no human value. Sponsorship is an act of love whereby the gift of life is made to shine and be honored. It is a lifelong skill that none perfects but all can benefit from.

III

THERAPY METHODS

6

THE REPARATION OF RELATEDNESS

A PROTOTYPE FOR SELF-RELATIONS WORK

> Healing complicates the system by opening and restoring connections among the various parts—in this way restoring the ultimate simplicity of their union. . . . The parts are healthy insofar as they are joined harmoniously to the whole. . . . Only by restoring the broken connections can we be healed. Connection is health.
>
> —*Wendell Berry, 1977*

> ONLY CONNECT! . . . Only connect the prose and the passion, and both will be exalted, and human love will be seen at its height.
>
> —*E. M. Forster, Howard's End*

SELF-RELATIONS suggests some basic interventions that might be helpful in psychotherapy. We saw in Chapter 4 how awareness might be returned to a felt sense of both a center and the relational field, so that a person experiences a relatedness to self, to others, and to a presence greater than the isolated ego. We examined in Chapter 5 some of the basic practices connected with the key principle of sponsorship of experience. This chapter elaborates a seven-step prototype for generating a relational self out of conflicting experiences.

The method is not a fixed prescription for how to do therapy with every person. Rather, it is a pattern that suggests coherent principles that can be applied differently for different people. Let me again reiterate the aesthetic base of self-relations: *the goal is to find a middle way between the alienation of intellectual discourse and the inflation of catharsis or regression*. The client should be helped to stay in the present while also feeling a variety of experiences via the somatic self. To allow for the emergence of this relational self, a felt connectedness between therapist and client must be developed and maintained throughout the application of the technique. *If you don't feel it, don't use the model.* This is difficult to convey in writing, but crucial to understand in practice. Based in part on the legacy of Milton Erickson, a main focus of the method is to gently open bodymind circuits, to reconnect the language of the cognitive self to the rhythms and knowledges of the somatic self. It should be used with a gentle rather than a hard precision, with relational grounding and nonverbal pacing. Many of the ideas, especially those of "aliens" and "neglected selves," will be unhelpful if not apprehended in the primary felt sense.

Step 1: Identify the problem

In this first step, the therapist seeks to identify what the problem is, where and when it is occurs, and what specifically happens that moves a merely unpleasant experience (e.g., I feel sad)

TABLE 6.1. STEPS IN THE BASIC SELF-RELATIONS METHOD

1. Identify the problem
2. Identify and somatically locate the neglected self
3. Activate and locate the cognitive self
4. Identify and differentiate from negative sponsorship
5. Connect cognitive self and (neglected) somatic self
6. Move back through problem sequence
7. Further practices for the relational self.

---

to an identity-defining symptomatic experience (e.g., I am depression). The therapist frame is something like, "*A funny thing happens on the way to this person becoming more of himself. What is it?*"

After receiving the client's general description of the problem, the therapist might ask something like: "*If I were accompanying you on a day (or week, or month) in your life, where and when would I see this problem occur?*"

If clients have difficulty getting specific or say something like, "It happens all the time," be gently persistent. You might ask, "When did it happen recently where it was really disturbing?" Asking about specific times and places moves the experience of the problem back into the "nowness" of the somatic self and thereby makes it available for change, so this step is crucial.

As the person describes a time when the problem occurred, the therapist slows down the processing to try to get a moment-by-moment, frame-by-frame description of the problem sequence. Frequently clients will rush through frames, jumping over important parts of the sequence. The therapist thus looks to slow things down to identify the sequential details of both exterior behaviors ("and then what did he do?") and interior experiences ("and what did you notice going on inside your body?" or "what were you aware of thinking then?").

A basic idea guiding the therapist is that at some point the client's neglected self is activated, which prompts him to leave the reality of the present moment and become trapped in the isolation and fixed understandings of the disconnected cognitive self. For example, say a person experiences his boss getting angry, which triggers a neglected self of fear in the person. The person tries to shut down these feelings and thereby loses connection to the present moment. Automatic conditioned responses (e.g., fear, anger, withdrawal) take over and express themselves in previously determined ways. To paraphrase Watzlawick, Weakland, and Fisch's (1974) definition of a clinical problem, life moves from "one damn thing after another" to "the same damn thing over and over." This is the "break in belongingness" and "break in relatedness" that devolves a difficult, unpleasant experience into a symptom-producing problem.

We need to remember that the abandonment of the somatic

self was probably unavoidable at some earlier point. It was the best a person could do to protect himself in threatening circumstances in which no positive sponsorship was available, internally or externally. But this dissociation process may become conditioned, occurring even after the threat is removed or after the person has developed other resources. The symptom represents a return of the neglected self, and therapy represents a ritual space where this return can be welcomed and integrated. The legacy of abandonment may be replaced by a process of relational connection.

To make this reconnection, we need to identify the sequence of disconnection, the place in time where the person abandons himself. Here is an abbreviated example of this part of the interview with a client whose presenting complaint was general fear and anxiety:

Client: . . .well, I guess the last time I got anxious was this morning when my friend came over.
Therapist: Your friend came over . . . may I ask your friend's name?
C: Bill.
T: Bill. And before Bill came over, how were you doing?
C: Okay. I was feeling okay that morning, just making some phone calls and stuff.
T: You were feeling pretty good and then this event with Bill started happening. When exactly, if you can just take a moment to relax and remember back, when exactly did you feel the first moment of disturbance? Was it before Bill came, or was it when he actually was there, that you began to feel the first suggestion that the problem of anxiety was going to happen? (*The therapist softens the tone to allow experiential accessing.*)
C: (*pauses to think*) Well, I began to feel a little nervous as soon as he walked in.
T: As soon as he walked in. And where were you?
C: I was sitting at my desk.

The therapist then asked a series of questions about the other furniture, what each person was wearing, what specifically was said, what was felt in the body at each point, and so forth. This procedure is an outgrowth of Ericksonian hypnotherapy procedures (see Gilligan, 1987), whereby associational questions are asked to revivify the problematic event, so that the experiential components of the sequence can be heightened and utilized. Again, the goal is to reconnect the descriptions of the cognitive self—that is, what's being talked about in the therapy conversation—with the experiences of the somatic self—that is, what is being experientially felt in the problem event—so that sponsorship may occur.

Step 2: Identify and somatically locate the neglected self

At some point in the problem sequence, a disturbing feeling develops in the client. This marks the appearance of the neglected self. To reiterate, a succinct formula for identifying the neglected self is to ask the client to fill in the following statement: "*If only I didn't do or experience (or could get rid of) X, then this really wouldn't be a problem.*" X marks the spot of the neglected self. For example:

- If only I didn't feel so inhibited, I would be successful.
- If only I didn't feel so angry, I could get on with my life.
- If only she wasn't so cold (and I didn't feel rejected as a result), our marriage wouldn't be such a problem.
- If only they weren't so corrupt, I could be happy.

The idea is that when this unacceptable experience or behavior arises, the person has to "leave town" or dissociate, because the identified stressor activates a "fight or flight" response in which a person loses connection to his center and to the field, leaving him in a reactive mode. *This is where the break in relatedness occurs, the neglected self develops, and symptomatic behavior is likely to arise.* Returning the neglected self into the relational self is thus the crucial step in healing. Three steps are helpful in this regard: (a) locate the somatic center, (b) identify an age, and (c) shift the pronoun.

Locate the somatic center

Ask the client: "*When the problem is present, where in your body do you most feel its center of disturbance (or discomfort)?*" Many people point immediately to their stomach, solar plexus, or heart area, even before conscious or verbal awareness has developed. If a person has difficulty understanding the question or developing a felt sense, it suggests he is too tense or too numb to sense the somatic self directly. Thus, inquiries about a felt sense of experience may elicit bewilderment or fear. In this not uncommon case, the therapist looks to find straightforward ways to develop relaxation and openness to self-connection. Any of the techniques discussed in the last several chapters may be helpful in this regard.

When you ask about somatic location, you might unobtrusively gently "scan" the person's body with your eyes, curious about where the "energy breaks" are. For example, you might sense where the person's body seems especially tense, or where it seems caved in or covered by crossed arms. A client often posturally protects the tender soft spot of the neglected self, and a therapist can become skilled in discerning this.

Once the neglected self has been somatically located, the therapist opens awareness to the corresponding somatic center within himself. For example, if the client describes a tight fear in his chest, the therapist might open his own heart center and be open to being with that fear. As we discussed in Chapter 5, the energetic felt sense of a somatic center should be distinguished from the emotional content held within that center. Thus, a person may sense both an open feeling in his heart and an experience of fear that is being held within that heart space. By opening his own centers to the client's experience, the therapist offers a temporary "holding space" for the neglected self of the client. This can help the client learn to sponsor and transform the same difficult experiences within his own somatic centers.

A major purpose of somatically locating the neglected self is to bringing a person back into the reality of the present moment. As the neglected self is distinguished in the time and space of "now," a more helpful relationship may be formed with it, as well as with the somatic self in general. (Remember, oppression or relational disconnection shuts the person off from the entire field, not just a part of it. This is the ultimate price paid for living in fear or hatred.) A specific advantage of localizing the neglected self is that it reduces generalized anxiety and agitation in a client. If an experience has no place to rest in a person's somatic self, it often is experienced as "free-floating" or rapidly shifting feelings that destabilize attention and undercut confidence. The amorphous quality of the unsponsored neglected self feels overwhelming. When it is given a place within a somatic center, its shape and form become more defined (although changing over time) and sponsorship becomes possible.

Identify an age

The somatic self has many identities and many ages. In fact, through its center in the body flows a progression of different archetypal forms. The neglected self is the limited version of the somatic self that occurs when a psychological experience being processed is arrested, its form fixed and "frozen in time."[1] The neglected self is typically experienced as an out-of-control feeling in the body (e.g., fear, helplessness, anger) that must be ignored, denied, repressed, or otherwise disconnected. To bring sponsorship and hence human value to it, the therapist somatically locates it and then identifies an age associated with it. This can by done by asking: *"If you were to let a number come to mind that represents an age for that (feeling) in your (identified somatic location), what number do you become aware of?"* The language here is somewhat hypnotic, and the question is delivered with a gentle but focused attention. Some straightforward relaxation suggestions may be given to help a person to "just let it happen."

[1] Again, the general idea is that experiences represent life moving through the bodymind. In order for an experience to become a memory or learning (to move from "now" to "then"), it must pass through multiple levels of processing—e.g., sensation, perceptual, cognitive, motor—to "metabolize." If the experience is too overwhelming or threatening—as in a biological or psychological trauma—neuromuscular lock "arrests" the processing and holds it in the somatic self as a separate state-dependent chunk of experience. Reintroduction of the trauma cues may reactive it. In addition, relaxation will release it, as it suggests that the danger is over and the processing of the experience may complete itself. This is why it is so hard for trauma survivors to relax: it activates the trauma. Hopefully, therapy can provide the context and tools to integrate the experiences into completed learnings.

Whatever age emerges, the therapist acknowledges it and senses it within the client. That is, *the client is two psychological ages at the time of the symptom: his present age (the cognitive self) and an earlier age (the neglected self).* As we saw in the "Who are you?" exercise of the last chapter, the capacity to hold both is the basis for developing the relational self.

In sensing the earlier age of the neglected self, remember that this age can and will change. It is important not to literalize and reduce a person's somatic self to a "frightened three-year-old." *This is precisely the mistake that the client has unwittingly made.* The therapist seeks to find ways to communicate that, while every age, every emotion, and every psychological form visit a person, a given one stays until it is accepted and sponsored. Acceptance allows release, and release allows new psychological ages and identities to emerge.

Shift pronoun from "it" to "he" or "she"

The central question in a psychological relationship—whether it be intrapersonal or interpersonal—is whether the "other" is regarded as an "it" or a "thou." Self-relations looks to move the neglected self from an "it" that needs to be controlled or otherwise disregarded to a "thou" that may be accepted. For example, say the client responded to the question regarding age with the number "three." The therapist might continue with: "*So . . . ("seeing" and sensing the person's neglected self as three years old) . . . he is three.*" In sponsorship terms, a compassionate delivery of this statement names and blesses the neglected self. The client typically responds with a deeply felt sense of tenderness and vulnerability. Such a response is experienced as coming from a place deeper than one's cognitive self. By connecting with gentle focus and openness, the therapist brings the experience of this neglected self into the relational field of human community.

As clients feel something awakening deep inside of them, they may experience some cognitive confusion, especially regarding the personal pronoun used to describe the neglected self. They may ask, "What do you mean, *he*?" The self-relations therapist responds by sustaining the nonverbal connection with the neglected self while having the following sort of conversation with the client's cognitive self:

Therapist: Well, if I'm hearing you correctly, you're saying that when the problem develops, one of the things that happens is you get an intense unpleasant feeling centered in your body that doesn't feel like it's coming from you or even belongs to you. It doesn't feel like your normal, everyday self is connected to the feeling. It's coming from someplace other than your regular sense of self. Is that right?

Client: Yes.

T: And if I'm hearing correctly, it seems that one of the most disturbing things is that when that feeling develops, somehow it feels like you disappear or disconnect and feel out of control, is that right?

C: Yes.

T: So I guess an important question is this: if that response isn't coming from your normal self, who is it and where is it coming from? (*brief pause to let this sink in*) There's obviously a lot of ways of talking and thinking about it, and certainly the more traditional way is to think of that experience that comes from deep inside of you as an "it" that has no meaning, that should be ignored or destroyed or gotten rid of. . . . I don't know who taught you that way of thinking about your experience . . . but it seems, if I'm hearing you correctly, that you've tried that approach many times and it hasn't worked . . . the bad feelings keep coming back over and over, more and more . . . so perhaps it might be helpful—not more true, but more helpful—to consider that the feeling belongs to *him*. . . to another aspect of you that is listening even right now. . . . *He* has his own feelings, his own thoughts and images, his own way of listening. . . . He's been ignored for a long time. . . . Others may have tried to get rid of him, to curse him, to ignore him, to hurt him . . . but it didn't work: he's alive and he's here . . . and the great thing is that it doesn't seem like you're able to deny him any longer. . . .

To make such communications effective, the therapist must be relationally empathic. The therapist touches the tender soft spot of the somatic self in the same way that a poet, a caring parent, a orator, or an Ericksonian hypnotherapist would naturally seek to do. Touching the center activates the proper experiential reference. Until this happens, the idea of a neglected self seems like psychobabble.

The therapist can further elaborate this idea that the symptomatic feelings represent the beingness of an other self that lives within each of us. If this idea of an "otherself" seems strange, remember that it is the basis for much artistic expression. An artist feels, listens to, and draws upon the "unconscious" to guide him. In the art of developing personhood, the same challenge exists: to realize and relate with the gift of inner life that lives in the soul of the somatic self. By locating and naming this archetypal presence, we transform a symptom into a creative act.

Step 3: Activate and locate the cognitive self

One of the great dangers (for both therapists and clients) in orienting to the neglected self is identifying with it. A person may become mired in a depressive sadness, sure it will never end, or grow addicted to righteous anger and rage, or regressively lock into a withdrawn fearful state. None of these identifications with the neglected self is helpful if sustained. The goal in self-relations is to access the neglected self without losing connections with the cognitive self and its perspectives and skills.

Accessing the cognitive self is especially helpful when a client seems to be getting overwhelmed by the neglected self. This is akin to a systematic desensitization method in which the painful stimulus (the neglected self) is progressively paired with a positive image (a competent cognitive self). To access the cognitive self, a less hypnotic, more straightforward, but still engaging nonverbal style is helpful. The client may be asked about his *present* age:

T: So *he* is three . . . (*Therapist connects with and silently holds the neglected self with nonverbal empathy, then releases gently.*). . . and by the way, how old are *you*? (*addressing the cognitive self*)

C: (*orients a bit from feeling of absorption*) Me?

T: Yes, you (*smiles, shifts in chair to a slightly faster tempo, and points to client*). He's three (*pointing to client's stomach*), but you—the you looking at me from behind your eyes, your regular self, how are you?

C: Well, I'm 43.

T: Yes . . . (*looks at client and senses him straightforwardly as a 43-year-old man with resources and competencies*) Yes, I can see that *you* are a 43-year-old man . . . and by the way, can you tell me what's the best thing about being 43 compared to three?

Most people say that the best thing about their present age is that they have more freedom and more ability to choose. *This reveals that the present age carries the capacity to sponsor the neglected self, though this is not clear to the client yet.*

To develop further connections with the present-age cognitive self, the therapist might ask a person about his work, present family and friends, interests, and so forth. These constitute associational "anchors" to the cognitive self that may be used to counterbalance the neglected self at any point in the conversation.

For example, say the therapist is talking with a client. The client is experiencing some sadness but is able to stay relationally connected. After a few minutes, the client seems to slide into a more intense, regressive sadness. To reorient the person to relational connection, the therapist might shift attention to the cognitive self by asking, "And by the way, what do you like to do best to enjoy yourself?" *Even when talking with the cognitive self, however, the therapist looks to sustain an underlying connection with the somatic self*; this is the relational holding of two identities discussed in the previous chapter. The shift to the cognitive self can disrupt the tailspin of the neglected self and restabilize attention to the present. After a few minutes, attention might shift back to the sadness.

The point is not to hold the person back from feeling, but to examine experience within a sustained relational connection to self, others, and the field. When these relational connections are broken, experience will be sensed and expressed in self-devaluing ways. Thus, the therapist's task is to ensure that experience is processed within a relational context. Shifting attention between cognitive and somatic selves is a helpful skill in this regard. Remember, of course, that the description given here is the prototype; many variations can and should be developed

Step 4: Identify and differentiate negative sponsors

We have identified in previous chapters two basic forms of negative sponsorship: (1) external sponsors who alienate a person from self, others, and life; and (2) self-intoxicating inductions a person has developed. We will explore each of these in turn.

Identifying and externalizing alienating sponsors

A major obstacle to activating or maintaining the cognitive self is the presence of alienating ideas. Remember the idea behind the concept of aliens: we are influenced by many people and sources. Some bless and awaken the tender soft spot, others curse and numb it. In traumatic situations, a person is invaded by alienating influences that imprint life-denying ideas: "You're stupid," "You are always going to mess up," "It's your fault," "You're no good," and so forth. These alienating ideas may negate the value and worth of a person's somatic experience, so a person cannot "be with" the experiences emerging from her center. Each time a feeling arises, the person under negative sponsorship rejects, ignores, and otherwise violently responds to it.

Therapists may sense the presence of aliens when clients disconnect during work. A client may without warning withdraw, become critical of self or others, or look frightened. Such "breaks in relatedness" signal that the alienating ideas have "taken over" the person. *The road to recovering the soul is landmined with aliens.* That is, as a person attends to his tender soft spot, he is met with threats that claim that if he really allows himself to know that feeling, something terrible will happen. In examining this issue, clients have discovered beliefs, for example, that if they really relaxed, they would go to bed and never get up; that if they attended to the their own needs, nothing would ever get done;

that if they ceased from compulsive doing, the whole world would pass them by and leave them "in the dust"; and that, if they didn't perform extraordinarily, they would literally disappear from the face of the earth. A person may recognize such beliefs as irrational but still be dominated by them.

The hope in self-relations is that a person may be liberated from such alienating ideas. As the Chilean poet Pablo Neruda (1969) wrote:

> If we were not single-minded
> about keeping our lives moving,
> and for once could do nothing,
> perhaps a huge silence
> might interrupt this sadness
> of never understanding ourselves
> and of threatening ourselves with
> death.

Negative sponsors may be identified and challenged in many ways. My own style often seeks to combine seriousness, mischievousness, and empathy. The following is an interchange with a client who was struggling with sadness. Each time he touched on the feeling, he shut down and became self-critical.

T: As we're talking about your experience, I'm wondering who *else* is talking to you about your experience.
C: What?
T: Who *else* is talking to you right now?
C: (*a bit bewildered*) What are you talking about?
T: (*serious but slightly playful*) Well, it seems that as we were talking, you began to touch upon some important experience . . . you started to look a little sad and tender . . . and then something seemed to happen. I don't know what you felt inside, but from outside it looked like something inside of you shut down and you had to go away.
C: (*pauses, looks sad and then disgusted*) Well, yeah . . . I shouldn't feel that way. . . .
T: (*with intensity and a bit of anger*) . . . Yeah, that's right . . . *those guys* . . . (*client's self-absorption is disrupted*) . . . the ones who are telling you that you shouldn't feel that way.

C: (*a bit bewildered*) What do you mean, those guys?

T: Well, where did you ever get the idea that those are *your* voices? (*some mischievousness is added to the blend*)

C:. Well, who else could they be?

T: (*with mock somberness*) Well, maybe you're possessed by aliens.

C: Aliens? (*looks at therapist, not sure if he's kidding or serious, but intrigued. Both therapist and client laugh for a moment.*)

T: (*maintains somberness with a touch of a twinkle, imitates a detached scientist*) I'm afraid so. . . . My professional opinion is that you're possessed by aliens. . . . (*pauses, then smiles gently. Both therapist and client burst out laughing. The spell is momentarily broken. Therapist shifts back into his normal mode.*) I'm only half kidding, because it seemed like when we were just talking, all of a sudden you weren't quite present. It seemed like some other presence came and you had to leave, to withdraw, to go away. Did you feel that?

C: Yes . . . (*looks down and sighs*). I felt shame and self-hatred.

T: Yes, I saw that. (*Tone is gentle and compassionate.*) Are you aware of what those voices (or ideas) are saying about you then, or even right now?

C: They're saying it was my fault. (*looks a bit sad but still connected to therapist*)

T: That it's your fault. . . . Well, what I'm suggesting is that perhaps one of the worst applications of capitalism to psychological experience is the idea that all the voices that move through you belong to you. One of the most helpful things about practices like hypnosis and meditation is that they allow you to really study those voices. You find that some support you . . . they allow you to be more present, they allow your experience to be accepted and expressed. I would call those your voices.

Other voices, you may find, make you go away. When they come, you have to leave. You feel smaller, less alive, unloved, and guilty. (*Client nods.*) So the question is, Are they really your voices? Do they really represent *you*? You could say they're your voices. But it sure doesn't seem like it to me. (*Therapist pauses and looks gently, with a mixture of compassion, seriousness, and a dash of mischievousness.*) I think you're possessed by aliens. (*pause to let imagination open and feeling develop*) . . . I'm partly kidding, of course, because it's hard to deal with your life without at least a little bit of humor . . . (*tone shifts to more tender sobriety*) but I'm also quite serious in suggesting that whatever happened to you, you got invaded by some stuff that told you you didn't deserve to live or show your true self (*pause to deepen connection*) I think those voices are wrong. I think they're alienating you from your self. (*long pause*) If you are possessed by aliens, there's a way out.

C: (*a bit entranced and teary-eyed*) What's that?

T: (*with gentle empathy and resonance*) Letting your own presence touch and reconnect with that otherself inside of you . . . that otherself that is present and listening even now . . . that part of you that was wounded and had to be abandoned . . . but who is listening right now. . . . Because when the relationship between you and him (the neglected self) is disconnected or abused, a break in relationship occurs—the elevators stop going up and down, you're no longer playing with a full deck—and the aliens come. (*The client accesses the neglected self and the sadness returns. To retrieve resources, the therapist gently shifts tone to access the cognitive self.*) But there are other times when you feel that good connection between the cognitive stuff in the head and the feeling stuff in your belly—the elevators are going up and down. (*The therapist might ask about times when the client doesn't feel alienated— for example, the "ordinary experiences of self-transcendence" discussed in Chapter 3—to point out that sometimes the aliens aren't around. The suggestion can then be made that such experiences reflect times when there is a connection between the cognitive self, the somatic self, and the field. It is precisely during these experiences of the relational self that aliens are not present; thus, reconnection of the two selves within the field is the best antidote to alienation.*)

Many clients find the idea of "aliens" exceptionally helpful. Like a meditation technique where a person is taught to detach from the thoughts in one's mind, it helps to free a person from identifying with negative influences, thereby allowing reconnection to a calm "thinking center" in the belly. Again, the term is meant poetically and is designed to generate both lightness and seriousness, so the therapist needs to present it in such a context. The intent of naming aliens is not to give primary focus to them, but to differentiate and externalize them from a person's own voice. The more primary intention is the realization of the relational self.

Most of us may have a long history living under the influence of alienating sponsors. Freeing oneself from them is an ongoing process that takes time and commitment. A person may find it helpful to make a list of all the "alien" messages that tend to attack. He can then learn on a daily basis to detect them and replace them with ideas of positive sponsorship.

Another technique, somewhat humorous but effective, is to install an "a.d.u."—that is, an "alien detection unit"—in the therapy conversation. Every time it seems like the negative sponsors are "kicking in," the therapist might make a beeping sound, announcing something like, "Alert. Alert. Alert. Aliens approaching. Aliens approaching. On the lookout, humans, aliens approaching to negate self-worth. . . ." Since most of the time the alienation happens outside of conscious awareness, such announcements can help to break the descending spell and reorient attention. Straight talk about what negative ideas a person was sensing can then occur.

Name and challenge self-intoxicating patterns

As we have seen, the relational self may also be ruptured by self-intoxicating practices such as self-pity, grandiosity, whining, envy, jealousy, crankiness, self-criticism, and self-doubt. When such practices surface, working with the wounds of the neglected self becomes quite difficult. Thus, it is helpful to identify and challenge these self-negating practices. The last chapter provided an example of how that might be done. The intent in such relational processes is to develop tender sobriety: the tenderness to feel and open to each aspect of one's experience, and the sobriety to see a situation with clarity and a lack of sentimentality. Both are lost by self-intoxicating practices. The somatic self is numbed to real feeling as it is overwhelmed by pseudo-feeling, and the cognitive self is distorted by life-sapping ideas.

It is a delicate practice to challenge self-intoxication, precisely because it combines both hard and soft parts of the person: the hardness of anger and self-protection, and the softness of the wounded tender soft spot and the fear that the pain will worsen if touched. Thus, a therapist who is too soft in challenging such practices will often be overwhelmed by the client's anger, directly or indirectly expressed, while the therapist who is too hard or insensitive will trigger fear and withdrawal in the client. Thus, the therapist needs to combine complementary ways of being in challenging self-intoxication: seriousness and mischievousness, Warrior and Lover energies (with a little wizardry thrown in on the side), challenging and yielding, immovable yet compassionate, soft yet intense.

For example, say a client is complaining about how nobody understands him. His demeanor has the feel of an old program that has been repeated in therapy for years. The therapist finds himself bored or angry or scared, without really knowing why. (Usually this means that the therapist, by virtue of being in the same field as the client, has absorbed and is under the influence of the same aliens that are attacking the client. Thus, noticing such interior responses may be helpful to the therapist's diagnostic process, provided he takes full responsibility for such processes.) We might say that the neglected self of fear (or anger) is being poisoned by the cognitive practices of self-pity.[2] If the therapist simply sympathizes with the client, he is likely to get hooked into a long-term pattern of placating the person's suffering, with nothing ever changing. Every therapist is painfully familiar with getting caught in this trap. But only challenging the client, demanding that he "just grow up" and "do something," will not be very helpful either.

Thus, the therapist must be sympathetic and challenging, open-hearted but sober at the same time. We saw in the last chapter how this can be done by directly naming the self-intoxicating

[2] As one of my aikido teachers is fond of telling his students, "You're working against yourself." Self-intoxicating practices work against the self. They numb or disconnect the life energy of the somatic self and deepen self-hatred and despair. Thus, therapists must work skillfully to disrupt and challenge such practices in loving and effective ways.

practice and then holding the relational connection while intense conversation develops about it.

There are, of course, other ways to defuse self-intoxicating inductions. One is to simply ask about your responses in each moment: *does this bring me closer to, or further away from, my center?* For example, if you're criticizing yourself or another person, or complaining about something, just notice its effect on your relationship to your center. Does it strengthen it or weaken it? Then notice how you are when you see that you've weakened your center. Does your response to that realization—for example, criticism or disappointment—bring you closer to or further from your center? As this question is repeatedly applied, it becomes clear that *most attempts to change our experience actually take us further from our center.*

In doing self-relations work it also becomes clear that attentiveness to one's center is far more relevant to happiness and productivity than any intellectual analysis of who's "right." Losing a connection to your center, you become reactive rather than responsive. Connecting with your center, you become capable of effective relational thinking and acting. When you find yourself engaging in practices that lead you away from your center—for example, when I hold a resentment, I forget about my center—you can use the attentional practices outlined in Chapter 4: breathing with awareness, relaxing, centering attention, softening attention, opening attention, and clearing attention. You can then simply ask what needs to be sponsored in your experience, and use any techniques from Chapter 5 to do so. No one ever graduates from this process, but it does become much easier to integrate into your everyday life. The issue gradually changes from being right to being alive, present, and helpful.

Step 5: Connect cognitive self and neglected (somatic) self

When a person's consciousness is not subjugated by negative sponsorship, it is free to reestablish the generativity of the relational self. The present model uses a scaling technique to identify the intensity level of the neglected self, the cognitive self, and the spirit of connection between them:

1. On a scale of 1 to 10, where 1 is the low end and 10 the high end, how much do you feel the presence of your neglected self in your (solar plexus) right now? Just let a number come to your mind.
2. On a scale of 1 to 10, where 1 is the low end and 10 the high end, how much do you feel the presence of your cognitive, everyday self in your head (looking out from behind your eyes) right now? Just let a number come to your mind.
3. On a scale of 1 to 10, where 1 is the low end and 10 the high end, how much do you feel a feeling of connection between the cognitive self in the head and the neglected self in the (belly)? Just let a number come to mind.

The goal here is to foster a felt sense of each relational component. Once this has developed, the therapist might ask if the client would like to experiment with lowering or raising the intensity value 1 or 2 points to see what happens (see Gilligan & Bower, 1984). For example, if the cognitive self is a 5 and the neglected self an 8, the client will often feel out of control. By going inside and gently "shifting knobs on the intensity controls," the cognitive self might be moved to a 7 and the neglected self to a 6. This small change in relative values can often make a significant difference in the person's overall quality of experience.

When asked about the level of connectedness between the two selves, some clients will look blankly, as if the idea of such a connection is entirely new. This is often the case: *the cognitive self and neglected self frequently have little or no history of coexistence.* When the person is absorbed in his cognitive self, the somatic self is ignored and forgotten. When his somatic self intensifies (e.g., during times of identity-related events, such as life transitions and symptoms), the cognitive self disconnects and is replaced by alienating influences. (Remember, aliens can only come in when you leave. You always have "first dibs" on sponsorship of the somatic self.) The goal of self-relations is to examine what happens when a person feels a relational connectedness between the selves. This is a structural description of wholeness, intimacy, love, and cooperation.

If a client has trouble feeling or connecting with the neglected self, simple suggestions to relax, center, and soften attention can help develop a felt sense. If he rejects the neglected self–for example, a person might say that the fear he experiences has no value and that he should just "grow up"–further work with alienating presences might be done. One approach I often use is to ask the client how he would respond to someone else feeling such fears. For example:

T: Do you think it would be helpful if when he (*the neglected self*) experiences that fear, he could feel your presence and support?

C: (*tightens up*) No! No way. He doesn't deserve any recognition. He should just get over it and grow up.

T: Hmmm . . . (*softens and pauses*) . . . Do you have children?

C: No.

T: Do you know any kids that you really like?

C: Yeah, I have a little eight-year-old niece.

T: A little niece. What's her name?

C: Arianna.

T: Arianna. . . . Do you like spending time with Arianna?

C: Yeah, a lot.

T: Well, I'm wondering . . . if you were around when Arianna was scared about something or another—because if you're around a person, they're going to get scared at some point— what would you say? What would you do? Would you punish her? (*This is said in a soft, intense voice.*)

C: (*His attention is absorbed.*) No, of course not.

T: Why not?

C: Well, she doesn't deserve it.

T: Yes, I see that you wouldn't punish her . . . (*silent absorption*). . . . Would you yell at her and tell her she's a bad person?

C: No, of course not.

T: (*pauses to silently be with this statement of integrity*) . . . Yes, I see that you wouldn't do that. What *would* you do?

C: (*speaks softly, with feeling*) . . . Well, probably just let her know that it was all right, that everything was going to be okay.

T: (*pauses to note this feeling of compassion in the client*) . . . Yes, I can see that. . . . How about if it was some other kid? Would you do the same thing?

C: Yes. (*This is again said with soft intense feeling.*)

T: (*silent absorption with this state*) . . . Yes, I can see that. That you feel that no person deserves violence or neglect, and that each person deserves respect and attention (*pauses to let it sink in*). So I guess the important question is (*silent pause to absorb with client*) are you a person too? . . . (*Client has tears in eyes; therapist softens and opens to further connection with client.*) The feeling you're having right now says that you are . . . the feeling that is coming from deep inside of you, the presence that's listening from deep inside of you, is awakenning. . . . Now I know that different people in your life rejected him or ignored him, told him he wasn't important or even that he didn't exist, but he didn't go away. . . . He's still here, and he's listening now. . . . Sometimes he's scared, and sometimes he's happy. . . . Sometimes he's shy, and sometimes he's outgoing . . . he's going to be alot of different things, a lot of different ways. . . . The real question is . . . how can *you* be with him?

This sort of conversation is designed to touch and bring awareness to the neglected self that is at the heart of a person's symptom. Typically there has been no human presence that has blessed and acknowledged this core experience, so it literally has no human identity. By sponsoring it, a person may begin to feel its deep value.

As the client opens to the relationship between his cognitive self and neglected self, he may be invited to gently close his eyes and deepen the telepathic link.

When the felt or "telepathic" sense of connection is made, the person will often look remarkably different. A sense of deep beauty and calm often imbues his being. He feels aware of but not identified with each self. This is not the cognitive self controlling the somatic self, or the "executive self" controlling a part of the self, or the "adult" controlling the "inner child." It is a felt spirit that connects the two selves, revealing not only their interdependence but also the relational field that constitutes an intelligence greater than either of them. This relational self may not last very long in the person's experience, but it marks an experience that the person can learn to return to over and over again. The real work and joy of life now begin.

Step 6: Return to original problem sequence

Since a problem degrades into a symptom when a sustained break in relatedness occurs, a reparation of the break will allow a person to move though a problem sequence without becoming symptomatic. For example, in our opening example in this chapter a man became anxious and self-critical during an exchange with his friend. We might say that the course of a friendly conversation was disrupted by the accessing of a neglected self and its disconnection from the cognitive self. Once we have reconnected these selves, the person might be invited to close his eyes and in his imagination go back through the relational event, this time keeping the telepathic inner connection and noticing any differences that occur. The client might sense, for example, how when he feels the fear in his somatic self, he can offer sponsorship via his cognitive self. This will likely lead to a more successful navigation of the external event.

Step 7: Further work

To reiterate the ancient lament: we abandon our souls a hundred times, no, a thousand times each day. Thus, this is not a "cure" but the beginning of a tradition of being relationally connected regardless of circumstance. Much practice is needed, and the therapist can talk with the client about how he can continue to nurture this tradition. Further self-relations work might occur; practices of meditation might be developed; specific conversations may need to occur with certain people; and so on. The realization is made that we cannot hope to never disconnect; in fact, we learn to accept that we check out and leave ourselves many times each day.[3] As we accept this as a given for each person, we can also grow stronger and more gentle in our commitment to "keep coming back" to the relational self and its goodness.

Summary

Life is one moment after the next, one thing after another, until it's not. It's not when some experience develops and a person has to "check out" of the present moment of life. This "break in relatedness" arrests a person's psychological movement in time, in effect having a person "spin his wheels" round and round in the same event, over and over again. As this happens, his responses are automated and self-devaluing, because as the self checks out the alienating influences check in. A person thus witnesses from the "near distance" of disconnected thinking his body feeling out of control and his experience subjugated by negative sponsors. The experience of this "symptomatic" relationship will continue until some sponsorship is brought to touch and reconnect with the disconnected experiences.

We have explored a seven-step method for developing this reparation of the relational self. The method seeks to pinpoint where and how the break in relatedness occurs, and then looks to achieve the three-part intervention of self-relations: sponsoring the neglected self, returning the cognitive self and activating its sponsorship capacities, and removing negative sponsorship to reestablish the relational field. As the relational self is regenerated, the difficulties of life may be successfully navigated.

In making this navigation, we are encouraged by the words of Kahil Gibran (1923) in *The Prophet*:

---

[3] A student of Morihei Ueshiba, the founder of aikido, was purported to have once said to his teacher, "Sensei, you never lose your center." Ueshiba replied that he lost his center as much as the next person, he just returned to it quicker. Thus, as we give up hope of "holding on" to perfection and always being centered, we open up to the "bamboo tree" flexibility of the moving center to which we may always return.

Among the hills, when you sit in the cool shade of the white poplars, sharing the peace and serenity of distant fields and meadows—then let your heart say in silence, "God rests in reason."

And when the storm comes, and the mighty wind shakes the forest, and thunder and lightning proclaim the majesty of the sky—then let your heart say in awe, "God moves in passion."

And since you are a breath in God's sphere, and a leaf in God's forest, you too should rest in reason and move in passion. (p. 51)

7

THE ARCHETYPAL SELF

WE GET BY WITH A LITTLE HELP
FROM OUR FRIENDS

> Last night, as I was sleeping,
> I dreamt—marvelous error—
> that I had a beehive
> here inside my heart.
> And the golden bees
> were making white combs
> and sweet honey
> from my old failures.
>
> Last night, as I was sleeping,
> I dreamt—marvelous error!—
> that a fiery sun was giving
> light inside my heart.
> It was fiery because I felt
> warmth as from a hearth,
> and sun because it gave light
> and brought tears to my eyes.
>
> Last night, as I slept,
> I dreamt—marvelous error!—
> that it was God I had
> here inside my heart.
>
> —*Antonio Machado, 1983*

When you use the voice as an instrument, you come across emotions that we don't have words for. You come across something like the memories of the human race in the voice.

—*Meredith Monk, in Erlich, 1996*

ONE OF THE MAJOR IDEAS of self-relations therapy is that we have two selves. Life flows through the tender soft spot of the somatic self, while it is understood, sponsored, and guided by the intelligence of the cognitive self. The relational self is realized from the conversation between these two minds.

Within the relational self, three basic types of relationship may occur. The first is *alienation,* where the cognitive self tries to dominate or ignore the somatic self. This may be expressed as denial, repression, intellectualization, ideological purity, and other forms of disconnection. The second is what Jung (1916/ 1971) called *inflation*, in which the cognitive self neglects or is overwhelmed by the archetypal patterns and feelings of the somatic self. This shows up in terms of acting-out, overidentification, addictions, and other "out-of-control" behavior and experience. The third is *relational*, wherein the person experiences and expresses an integrated sense of the two selves, as well as a connection to a larger field.

To develop this relational self, we must understand and work with the somatic self. This skill is central to any art, whether it be painting, parenting, dancing, doing therapy, growing up, or being in an intimate relationship. The somatic self is the local center of nature: it carries the rhythms and seasons of birth and death, darkness and light, calmness and storminess. Just as life dies and returns into the ground, experience is lived and then absorbed into the body. These experiences are not only individual but collective (ancestral) as well. As Eliot (1963, p. 189) remarked, it is "a lifetime burning in every moment/and not the lifetime of one man only."

Thus, working with the somatic self reminds us that we are constantly influenced by two histories: a history of the personal self (where we've been and what's happened in our particular life), and a history of the species or collective self. Jung (1919/ 1971) suggested that the latter is organized around universal themes, images, and relational patterns. These general patterns represent the challenges or ways of being central to each human life: for example, to love and receive love, to protect life and to maintain differences and boundaries, to heal wounds and change identity, and to give blessing and provide a place for each member of a community. The fact that each generation of human life has had to deal with these challenges has led to the development of psychological images and structures that are common to the human psyche. These are what we refer to as archetypes. Jung (1919/1971) observed:

> Archetypes are typical modes of apprehension, and wherever we meet with uniform and regularly recurring modes of apprehension we are dealing with an archetype, no matter whether its mythological character is recognized or not. . . . The collective unconscious consists of the sum of the instincts and their correlates, the archetypes. Just as everybody possesses instincts, so he also possesses a stock of archetypal images. . . . The archetype (or primordial image) . . . might suitably be described as the instinct's perception of itself. (p. 57)

Archetypes are especially evident in dreams, literature, art, war, and other basic human expressions. We see mastery of archetypal process in basketball's Michael Jordan (the Warrior/Hero), psychotherapy's Milton Erickson (the Magician/Healer), and religion's Mother Theresa (Lover/Healer). We see archetypal process in trance, marriage encounters, drug-taking, religious ceremonies, and sex. What makes these persons or processes archetypal is that, in certain contexts, they reflect both a personal and universal meaning. They express not only themselves but also an experiential pattern found over and over again throughout the history of consciousness, usually cross-culturally. As we will see, there is significant value in seeing both a personal (individual) and transpersonal (collective) meaning in certain behaviors.

Archetypes are evident in psychological symptoms. As Jung (1957) remarked:

> We think we can congratulate ourselves on . . . having left the (archetypal) gods behind . . . but we are still as much possessed by autonomous psychic contents as if they were Olympians. Today

they are called phobias, obsessions, and so forth; in a word, neu-
rotic symptoms. The gods have become diseases; *Zeus no longer
rules Olympus but rather the solar plexus* (italics added) (par. 54)

Of course, archetypes do not always produce negative experiences. This chapter examines how archetypes may be recognized
and utilized as positive resources in therapy. For example, they
constitute an important basis for therapist-client communication,
as suggested by Erickson and Kubie (1940/1980):

> . . . underneath the diversified nature of the consciously organized
> aspects of the personality, the unconscious talks in a language
> which has a remarkable uniformity . . . so constant that the un-
> conscious of one individual is better equipped to understand the
> unconscious of another than the conscious aspect of the person-
> ality of either. (p. 186)

Thus, archetypal process may be seen to flow both within a person and between persons (e.g., therapist and client). The rest of
the chapter examines the relevance of this to the practice of psychotherapy. Some general ideas about archetypes are first over-
viewed. A model for identifying and working with the archetypal
resources inherent in a problem is then detailed. Finally, the therapist's use of archetypal modes of communication is examined.

Basic ideas about archetypes

Table 7.1 lists nine ideas about archetypes relevant to psychotherapy. We will explore each in turn.

1. The primary function of an archetype is to help a person develop as a human being

Life sends each person challenge after challenge to help her
realize her gifts and capacities. Many of these challenges are universal: our ancestors faced them, and their experiential learnings

---

TABLE 7.1. IDEAS FOR USING ARCHETYPES IN THERAPY

1. The primary function of an archetype is to help a person develop as a human being.
2. Each archetype has a deep structure and many possible surface structures.
3. The selection of an archetypal form is significantly influenced by cultural and personal biases.
4. Ontogeny recapitulates phelogeny: Each archetype has a developmental progression.
5. Each archetype has integrated and unintegrated forms.
6. The value of an archetype depends on its human sponsorship.
7. A person should not be reduced to or confused with archetypes.
8. Archetypes are especially active at times of identity change.
9. The goal of therapy is to sponsor the gifts of life sent to each of us.

---

and responses are constellated in their gifts of archetypal forms. These gifts can help us meet these timeless challenges.[1]

An example of an archetypal challenge is developing the experience of communion, of becoming part of something bigger than our individual self. It is something each person is instinctually called to do. In his classic book, *The Art of Loving*, Erich Fromm described how, if this universal calling is not satisfied via the skill of loving, a person is driven to achieve it in less effective ways— for example, joining a cult, becoming a fascist, drugs, sex, rock 'n' roll, or other forms of fundamentalism.

There are, of course, numerous other archetypal challenges. For example, the model we will explore in the next section distinguishes four archetypal energies: Lover, Warrior, Magician/ Healer, and King/Queen. Some of the challenges represented by these archetypes include communion, passion, and acceptance;

---

[1] In a perhaps apocryphal story, Golda Meier (the former Prime Minister of Israel) and a rabbi were once talking. The rabbi noted that he was able to consult with fellow rabbis about very important decisions, and wondered whether Golda's position as leader of the country allowed her to have confidants. She replied that she consulted with two people on every important decision: her grandmother (who was no longer alive) and her granddaughter (who had not yet been born).

fierceness, commitment, and differentiation; healing, enchantment, and reframing; and blessing and finding place. These are just a few of the many universal aspects of being human.

The point here is that archetypal process flows through us, *especially at times of identity change.* When it does, we may feel "out of control," taken over by forces more powerful than our cognitive self. This can be an exhilarating experience, as when falling in love, or a terrifying one, as when a symptom develops. In the latter case, we feel frightened and do not understand why things are happening the way they are.

Self-relations therapy assumes that this is because symptomatic experiences are often archetypal in nature: they call us to transcend the boundaries of the cognitive self and become part of a deeper human experience. In this regard, an archetypal presence serves as a sort of sponsor for a person: it awakens her awareness to a presence inside of herself and the world, and guides her processes of developmental growth in that archetypal area. As we will see, at the same time it is important for the person to sponsor the archetype. This reciprocal sponsorship is a mark of a mature relationship.

Since the therapist sees the "other than conscious" force of the symptom as partly an archetypal gift, she sympathizes with a client's fears but also welcomes the symptom in terms of its potential. She assumes that the symptom represents the spirit of life wanting to help a person grow. For example, the process of addiction may be regarded as an extraordinary instance of a person seeking communion with something bigger than herself (Zoja, 1989). The presence of this "Lover" archetype is enormous and is incredibly destructive, yet it carries the seeds of positive development. As we will see in the next section, the task of therapist is how to frame the symptomatic behavior in positive archetypal terms, such that a symptom becomes a solution.

2. Each archetype has a deep structure and many possible surface structures

To see a symptom as an archetypal solution, it is important to realize that each archetype is a general pattern that may be expressed in an infinite number of specific ways. Like DNA or a therapeutic story, it constitutes general suggestions, not specific commands. Thus, while we may be compelled to express archetypal patterns, how we do so is quite variable. For example, you might ask, "*Whom do you think of as an example of the Lover archetype?*" It could be a movie star, a person in real life, a family member, a mythological character, and so forth. There are many possibilities, each one bearing strengths and weaknesses. One of my first (and most enduring) examples of the Lover archetype was my mother. When I was a child, she personified the conservative Catholic martyr mother, devoted to loving everybody but herself. This "love others but not oneself" principle was adopted in my own life.

In a similar way, a client's understanding or image of an archetype might be very limiting. For example, a successful businesswoman suffered through a series of very abusive relationships. She couldn't understand why she stayed with such low-grade characters. As we examined her images of what a lover looked like, both female and male, it became clear that she had a fixed understanding from cultural and familial learnings of a female lover as an abused, unworthy character. As I complimented her deep connection to the force of love, I also gently challenged her to find other, more nurturing ways to express and bring this force into relationships.

This is a common strategy in self-relations work: (1) examine the symptomatic pattern for evidence of archetypal pattern; (2) distinguish the specific (negative or limiting) form of the archetypal pattern from its general positive function; (3) compliment the person on her connection to the general positive function; and (4) develop and encourage other (more helpful) specific forms to express this general function. The general idea is that a person needs multiple images for each archetype, so that flexibility and responsiveness to changing circumstances may occur.

3. The selection of an archetypal form is significantly influenced by cultural and personal biases

For example, sexism or racism may limit the range of archetypal content readily available to a person from a given gender or race. Thus, a person may be compelled to express the archetypal process of the Warrior, for instance, but have available only destructive examples of that archetype.

In one case, Bill was an intense young man in his twenties who had suffered horrible violence at the hands of his father. Now he practiced the martial art of aikido with great conviction, seemingly guided by a Warrior image that was brutal and unforgiving. Fortunately, he trained under a high-ranking Japanese sensei (teacher) who was a remarkably gentle and light-spirited man. One day, during a class dealing with knife attacks, Bill responded to his partner's attack with an incredibly hard throw. The training partner fell to the floor hard, his body crumpled so awkwardly that Bill was having a hard time applying the appropriate arm-lock pinning technique. As he struggled with his partner, the sensei walked over from across the room, scratching his head with curiosity. "What you doing? What you doing?" he asked playfully but intently. Bill answered sharply, "I'm trying to pin the man, sir!" The sensei looked puzzled, scratched his head again, then said, "You have your wallet, run! Run!" He threw up his hands, as if any true Warrior could see that was the right thing to do, and sauntered off.

Bill was left with his mouth open, reeling from this hypnotic confusion technique. After all, he was committed to becoming a true Warrior, and here was this true Warrior suggesting that the best thing to do would be to get out of harm's way. Bill had no card in his mental Rolodex of Warrior images to match his sensei's suggestion, yet he had great respect and admiration for the sensei. His rigid behavior began to soften after that, and his understanding and expression of the Warrior archetype seemed to mature significantly.

The social constraints on archetypal understanding should not be underestimated. *Life may demand that a person express each archetypal energy, but social constraints may severely limit how a person responds to these demands.* The result is that instinctual patterns are often expressed in distorted or limited ways. Therapy may help liberate a person from such constraints, allowing for the development of more satisfying forms of archetypal expression.

In other words, a goal in working with archetypes is to bring them under the mindfulness of the client, away from their mindless misuse by other systems. Thus, a person may feel the archetypal urge to the Warrior qualities of fierceness, penetration, and commitment. But she may live in a society where women are not allowed such qualities and men are encouraged to express them via images of dominance and physical violence. Thus, the woman might turn these energies against herself in a self-attack of criticism and subjugation of her body, while the man might translate them into dominating others. The therapeutic work with archetypes would encourage both to examine the effects of such practices and to develop more respectful and satisfying understandings and practices.

The social exploitation of archetypes often reduces them to life-sapping stereotypes. As Carol Pearson (1989) has noted:

> . . . many of our socialization patterns are based on limiting stereotypes, but it is not possible simply to decide that they are not good for us and then ignore them. The *stereotypes* are laundered, domesticated versions of the *archetypes* from which they derive their power. The shallow stereotype seems controllable and safe, but it brings then less, not more, life. The archetype behind it is full of life and power. (pp. xix–xx)

Thus, a stereotype occurs when an archetype has its energy drained and its autonomy denied. When reconnected with a somatic center and the relational field, an archetype may once again become life-affirming.

4. Ontogeny recapitulates phylogeny; each archetype has a developmental progression

In addition to social and cultural constraints, developmental factors influence the form of archetypal expression. Jean Houston (1980, 1987) has brilliantly described how the psychological development of an individual repeats the psychological development of the species. This is a psychological version of the biological principle of "ontogeny recapitulates phylogeny." Thus, for example, the archetypal force of the Warrior, with its related qualities of fierceness, focus, commitment, and self-protection, will appear throughout a person's life, but its form will change over time.

Houston suggests that the developmental progression of this Warrior energy will reflect its development over centuries of human history. At first, the archetypal form is undeveloped or immature. For example, a one-year-old's Warrior expressions appear as temper tantrums, perhaps akin to the Neanderthal stage of Warriorship. As a person matures and receives sponsorship, her understanding and expressions of that same archetypal energy will become more civilized. A child growing up with guidance may learn to manifest her Warrior energy in ways of service to the community (see Fields, 1991). It is, of course, a long road from early civilization to its more advanced forms. (Watching my four-year-old daughter, she seems at about the developmental stage of Attila the Hun when it comes to expressing her anger with friends. But we're working with it!)

The progression of an archetypal form is often not linear. Trauma or other stresses may cause regression in a developmental form. A person may express relatively mature forms of an archetype in most situations, but then show immature, less developed forms in areas of a symptom. For example, one client showed mature Lover qualities in his work as a therapist, but was extremely needy and greedy in his relationship with his wife. Again, a major goal of therapy is to identify an immature or unhelpful form of archetypal expression implicit in a symptom, then apply the skills of sponsorship to help transform it into a more mature, positive expression.

5. Each archetype has integrated and unintegrated forms

An archetypal expression may be constructive or destructive, depending on the relation of the person to the archetype. For example, the constructive aspects of the King/Queen archetype include blessing, finding place, and creating a system where everyone belongs. The dark side includes curses ("you exist only to serve me") and oppression.

6. The value of an archetype depends on its human sponsorship

The main determinant of whether an archetype is integrated is its relation to human presence. Each time an archetypal form enters a person's somatic self, it may be accepted or rejected. That is, it may be touched by human presence and brought into the relational self or ignored or rejected and hence held outside of the sphere of the relational self. (This decision may be largely unconscious and based on various cultural, familial, and other conditioning factors.) Acceptance and sponsorship allow a more positive and mature form to develop; rejection tends to turn it into a negative and devolved form. *Thus, the value of the archetype is not inherent; it is determined in each moment by the persons present in the relational field.*

For example, a major function of the Magician/Healer archetype is to enchant and shift attention. This expression could be positive: a person might go into a therapeutic trance (an archetypal process of healing) and transform her understanding of a problem. Or it could be negative: the same person might use her "enchanting skills" to deceive herself or others. In both situations, the person is expressing the archetypal process of the Magician; the difference is whether she is expressing it within or outside of the relational self.

To express an archetype within the relational self, blessings and other forms of sponsorship are needed. To reiterate, blessings originally come from others in the community; then, as a person matures, they may also be self-administered. If an archetype arises within consciousness and is cursed, it will tend to play out as having no human value, e.g., as symptoms. Its form will be aesthetically ugly and its function perceived as dysfunctional or undesirable. This is where we start in therapy. As love and its skills of sponsorship relationally connect with an archetypal form, its form and function will begin to transform. *The touching of any psychological form with human presence begins a transformational process.* This transformational process may be aborted at any time by the withdrawal of positive sponsorship.

The idea of bringing sponsorship and love to the archetypal gifts from the psyche is especially important in contemporary times. It used to be that archetypal images were introduced into consciousness via traditions such as story-telling, dreams, art, ritual, and so forth. Increasingly, in our societal movement to the mythology of materialism, its lifestyle of consumerism, and its practice of advertising, archetypal images are introduced via television and other media. One need only glance at a young child watching television to see a context that promotes spectatorship rather than participation. Furthermore, the archetypal images are introduced by corporate "sponsors," with the clear intent of fomenting the agitated desire to consume products rather than to develop personhood and citizenry.

In such circumstances, it is easy to see the crucial contribution of human sponsorship to the value of archetypal images. When loving sponsorship is absent, as in the contexts of consumerism or fundamentalism, the result is addiction to fantasy, projection onto others, susceptibility to emotional manipulation, and ultimately depression ("crashing") into soulful emptiness. Archetypal processes become habituated, and the presence of human being is contracted or altogether lost. The relational self ceases to exist, and the archetype (in its depersonalized form) overwhelms the person. Examples of this include Madonna, Adolph Hitler, a depressed client, and an acting-out borderline client.

When sponsorship is negative—as it is in fundamentalism and consumerism—repression, dissociation, projection, despair, and other forms of disconnection are enacted. Authentic sponsorship means that both the cognitive self and the archetypal processes of the somatic self are equally active and cooperative. This is what art is about—whether the art of relationship, of therapy, of sports performance, or of parenting. Thus, self-relations seeks to promote harmony, balance, and cooperation between the cognitive and (archetypal) somatic selves.

7. A person should not be reduced to or confused with archetypes

We must always distinguish persons from archetypes. It is precisely the reduction of a person to a psychological form, archetypal or otherwise, that destroys the possibility of fresh, solid, and free experience. Archetypes are patterns or resources sent by the psyche to help a person on her journey; the role of the person in receiving, naming, holding, understanding, and expressing these archetypal forms is of primary importance. A person's success in achieving this reciprocal sponsorship of the archetypal (somatic) self and sponsoring self is what determines whether something is a problem or a solution.

Thus, we should be concerned with literalizing expressions such as "my inner child" or "my inner warrior." As Wilber (1995) has emphasized, archetypes may be expressed in pre-rational or trans-rational consciousness. In the trans- or post-rational context, a person holds the mythical image in an "as if" mode, feeling its vitality and messages but recognizing that he or she is not the image. If a person slips and identifies as the image, a regressive acting-out of a pre-rational structure will occur. A danger exists when a person doesn't have the flexibility to adjust a psychological form across contexts. For example, the way in which we express love to our children changes from moment to moment; its actual form arises out of the unique situation rather than from some rigid understanding of what love means. This rigidity is especially present when a person is identified with only one archetype, since a major characteristic of creative action is connection to complementary energies and truths. Thus, we hope that a person informed by the Warrior archetype, with its fierceness, focus, and intensity, may be equally informed by the Lover archetype, with its gentleness and acceptance. These energies combined make for a tender sobriety or a nonviolent fierceness. Because these crucial integrations are less likely in a pre-rational than a post-rational mode, it is important to know the difference between these contexts.

Another way to express this difference is that in pre-rational consciousness an archetype is taken on as a singular identity to be lived. You are sponsored by it, but it is not reciprocally sponsored by you. It is a frame of reference that is relatively unquestioned. In post- or trans-rational consciousness, on the other hand, an archetype is a deep somatic poem, one among many that fill a person with vitality and images. A trans-rational consciousness receives these different energies and then acts from the level of a person, not an archetype.

8. Archetypes are especially active at times of identity change

In normal times, the cognitive self is generally dominant in experience. It plans, works out details, maintains focus, and navigates through social understandings. But at the beginning and end of an identity cycle, or when trauma or significant failure hits, it is no longer business as usual. New ways of understanding and expressing oneself are needed. It is precisely at this point that archetypal process becomes dominant. *When a person can no longer navigate events via her present identity, the psyche sends archetypal material to help.*

In other words, in normal times a person has a frame of reference that is more or less helpful. She thinks of herself and the world around her in a certain way, and her frame helps her to develop this identity. When major life events or developmental passages occur, her old identity is no longer valid. She is between worlds, with her old self no longer quite helpful and her new self not quite developed. It is at these times that the cognitive self is impotent and the archetypal process of the somatic self must become dominant in order to allow a death and rebirth cycle. Thus, we look to welcome archetypal processes at times of great change.

9. The goal of therapy is to sponsor the gifts of life sent to each of us

When archetypal process becomes dominant, a person may feel frightened and engage in a fight-or-flight response: shutting down, using defense mechanisms, being overwhelmed with depression or anxiety, trying harder, etc. Most of these responses make matters worse, with each ensuing cycle of a repetition compulsion. At some point, the person may seek a therapist.

The big question is how a therapist regards and works with such "out-of-control" symptoms. Self-relations encourages sponsorship of the symptom through the skills of deep listening, acceptance, proper naming, boundary setting, skill building, blessing, encouraging, and loving. By approaching symptoms as unintegrated archetypes, we may practice the sponsorship skills needed to transform a problem into a solution.

A clinical model for working with archetypes

Table 7.2 shows a four-step model for working with symptoms as archetypes. To see how this approach works, we will use the quaterno model of the four archetypal energies shown in Figure 7.1: Lover, Warrior, Magician/Healer, and King/Queen.[2] As can be seen, each archetype is balanced by its complement, and each has an integrated and unintegrated form. The goal is to translate an unintegrated form into an integrated one.

The King/Queen provides blessings and a sense of one's place(s) in the social world; its dark side is tyranny and curses. It is the inner voice that tells you in the best way that you belong in the world, that you are special and have something important to contribute—or that you have no right to exist or no abilities or competencies or future.

Most people can identify at least one person in their lives who served as a positive King or Queen. For me, great blessings were given to me in childhood by my mother, my grandfather, and several teachers. Above all, Milton Erickson was a King to me, giving me blessing, seeing me in a deep way and conveying the message that there was a place for me in the world. Without such blessings, it is hard to feel present in the world.

TABLE 7.2. A FOUR STEP MODEL FOR WORKING WITH SYMPTOMS AS ARCHETYPES

1. Identify the archetypal energy present in a symptom
2. Compliment the person on the presence of the archetypal energy
3. Encourage the client to "do it more, do it better"
4. Develop new ways of understanding and expressing the archetypal energy.

---

[2] This quaterno model, modified from Moore and Gillette (1990), is not intended as an exhaustive model. For example, another model by Carol Pearson (1989) identifies six major archetypes: Orphan, Innocent, Wanderer, Martyr, Warrior, and Magician. While different archetypes may be added, the main point is that sponsoring symptoms as archetypal energies may help transform an enemy into an ally.

FIGURE 7.1. SOME GREAT ARCHETYPAL TRADITIONS: KING/
QUEEN, WARRIOR, LOVER AND MAGICIAN (ADAPTED FROM
MOORE & GILLETTE, 1990)

At the same time, curses are easy to come by. Messages such as
"you have no worth," "you're stupid," and "you exist only to
serve me" abound in relationships. Many of them get locked in
the somatic self and stick in one's identity.

The Lover deals with passion and communion. When unintegrated or abused, its dark side is addiction and co-dependence. Its
energies draw you to connect and join and surrender to something bigger than yourself. When not grounded within the relational self and balanced by complementary archetypes, it is expressed as addictive communion with drugs, food, people, or
some other pseudo Lover.

The Warrior energies are concerned with boundaries, fierceness, commitment, and service. They help you to declare your
values, your interests, your sense of self. They keep you focused
and committed in relationships. They detect bullshit, reflect attacks, and help you to fight for integrity and for your voice to be

heard and respected. When unintegrated, Warrior energies are expressed as rage, crankiness, criticalness, and invasion of others.

When I was growing up, my father carried the unintegrated energies of the Warrior in his drunken violence. When I was a teenager, the Vietnam war carried disturbing Warrior images. It is easy to see how my initial understanding of Warrior energy was very negative, and why I tried (with ultimate failure) to adopt the Beatles song "All You Need Is Love" as my self anthem. When I got married some years later, my denial of the Warrior archetype became a major problem. I could not work out differences in a fight: afraid of violence, I would withdraw into silence for days. Thus, I was forced to begin the long process of cultivating the crucial aspects of this energy.

The Magician/Healer energies focus on transformation (the death of one identity and the birth of another), enchantment, and healing. The dark side is deception and trickery, as well as the dark spells of symptomatology. You encounter these energies especially at times of identity shifts, during traumas, or in trance. Magicians know the paradoxical, symbolic, story-telling language of the underworld. Erickson was a beautiful example of the Magician archetype, all the way down to his physical wounding by polio as he approached adulthood (this is a classic mark of the healer in traditional cultures), purple outfits, story-telling, and hypnotic language. In unique ways, every good therapist is deeply connected to the Magician/Healer energies.

In its dark form, the Magician is into deception of self and other; it is a bullshitter, chameleon, distracter, seducer, and cheap reframer. Therapy, especially hypnosis, is very susceptible to this dark energy. Both therapist and client may believe that everything is changing (e.g., via a spectacular trance), whereas in fact nothing in the person's life is changing at all. Thus, the Magician must always be balanced by the sobriety of the Warrior and the tenderness of the Lover, as well as the King/Queen energy that senses the proper place of enchantment.

The important thing is that *none of these archetypes is you*. As Jung (1919/1971) repeatedly emphasized, the most important archetype is the self, which is always seeking to awaken into the world. When the self is sensed, the different archetypal learnings coalesce as unique expressions of you. You continue to integrate the powers of love into your life. You develop the Warrior skills of setting boundaries, declaring values, making commitments, cutting through deception, and fighting for integrity. You learn the Magician skills of persuasion, enchantment, reframing, storytelling, and navigating developmental transitions. You cultivate the inner King/Queen marriage that gives blessings to self and other, and you sense how each person or pattern has a place and fits in an overall order.

When these archetypal energies are not connected within the relational self, they continue to challenge you. You are left mired in their dark forms: addiction and anxiety, self-denigration, rage and boundary-breaking, and the dark trances of symptomatology. Thinking in terms of these archetypes can help therapists sense how even (or especially) when clients are caught in any of these processes, they are deeply engaged in some important archetypal process. By sensing what this process might be, the therapist may support a person in claiming it and expressing it with more variety, responsibility, and integrity.

To accomplish this, I have been using what might be called "listening questions" for each tradition. These are questions to be answered more by the somatic self than by the cognitive self. The therapist doesn't try to figure them out intellectually; instead, she holds the question in a quiet, attentive, and centered way while listening to the client. Let the answers come rather than trying to find them. As the poet Antonio Machado (1983) suggested:

> To talk with someone,
> ask a question first
> then—listen. (p.143)

Table 7.3 represents the listening questions used for the four archetypal traditions. As the therapist reflects on these questions, responses that arise are taken not as truth but as clues about how the symptom may be seen as a solution. The value of a description is entirely in the client's response. If the therapist's response awakens some deeper experiential response in the somatic self—a trance, an emotional feeling, a disruption—it's a keeper. If not, let go, center, listen, and try again. Once an archetypal presence is developed, further conversation keeps the client engaged at this

TABLE 7.3. LISTENING QUESTIONS FOR THE LOVER ARCHETYPE

Lover	Warrior
1. To whom/where is this person's passion or love connected? 2. From whom/where is love being withdrawn? 3. As this person connects with the inner Lover, what might his future look like?	1. This person is fighting for something important—what is it? 2. Where are more boundaries needed? 3. As this person connects with the inner Warrior, what might his future look like?
Magician/Healer	King/Queen
1. What major shift in identity is occurring? What is dying and what is being born? 2. Where are the unattended wounds that need to be addressed? 3. As this person connects with the Magician energies, what might his future look like?	1. What is this person's place(s) in the world? (That is, where and how is he special?) 2. What blessings are needed? 3. As this person connects to the inner King/Queen, how might his future be different?

experiential level, with the intent of transforming the negative form of the archetype into a positive, more helpful form.

To do this, the therapist communicates three general ideas:

1. You're up to something big! (*compliment*)
2. You can do it even "more and better." (*expand*)
3. As you continue to do it, many possible learnings will develop. (*suggest possibilities/open imagination*)

An alternative statement of these ideas is that (1) something is waking up within the person, (2) it is possible to effectively attend to this awakening process, and (3) this attention will result in reduced suffering and increased happiness.

For example, a male perpetrator of violence might be acknowledged as having big-time involvement in the Warrior archetype, albeit in its dark, destructive forms. Invitations to responsibility, as Alan Jenkins (1990) has called them, are then developed to encourage and challenge the person to identify and expand his images of an inner Warrior. (Many may be initially imaged as rageful fathers or Rambo-like sociopaths.) For example, the statement might be made:

> When it comes down to it, nothing and nobody is going to be able to make you change. Your connection with Warrior energy is just too big and too deep. There's nothing that can be done about it. My only question to you is, What the hell is worth fighting for? I don't know why you're wasting your time on this stuff, with all that Warrior energy so deep inside of you. What the hell is worth fighting for?

As more responsible, integrated Warrior energies are connected, they can be blended with those of the King (who is in charge of directing the Warrior) and the Lover (who softens and balances the Warrior). Again, the person is none of these archetypes, so you continue to talk directly with him and encourage him to "show up" in a responsible and self-connected way.

Another example is a person with suicidal thoughts. She might be seen as engaged in the death and rebirth cycle of the Magician tradition. In this way, the voice that says, "I don't want to live this life anymore," may be regarded as having great integrity, suggesting that some unworkable false self the person has identified with is dying. It is, of course, a highly dangerous situation, since the person (and the culture) usually interprets such ideas in terms of physical suicide, rather than psychological death. The challenge is to develop a ritual space that contains the person from physically acting out while making room for the deeper psychic process of death and rebirth. The therapist might say to the suicidal client something like,

> There's something inside of you that says a death is needed. I hear that voice and believe that voice. . . . I think it speaks with great integrity . . . something may indeed need to die inside of you.

When delivered in an experientially sensitive way, such a message absorbs the somatic self and relaxes a suicidal person, since it is often the first time someone has spoken directly to the relentless death-seeking voice and validated it as vital to self development. Further conversations seek to develop ways to allow this inner voice to help in a self-affirming though difficult psychic death process. Since the Magician energies are especially connected with altered states, ritual and trance are common features of this conversation.

As with any therapeutic process, the therapist works at each step of the process to ensure safety and maintain experiential absorption with the somatic self. The client's inner responses guide the action, but the therapist is responsible for creating a therapeutic context where new meanings and possibilities arise. Of course, many other techniques are used along with the archetypal processes. The goal in therapy is not to develop archetypes; it is to help a person live life in a more satisfying fashion.

In working with archetypes, we begin to see that they represent the complementary qualities of the relational self. The surrender and communion of the Lover blend with the agency of the Warrior to form the "agency-in-communion" of the relational self. The self-transformation of the Magician/Healer and the self-transcendence of the King/Queen form another self-relational expression. As Wilber (1995) remarked, these properties—agency, communion, dissolution, and transcendence—are central to any intelligent consciousness. None is superior; all are necessary. One therefore strives to find one's center in order to feel and integrate the shifting balance of these different energies.

The question is where to start, and then how to blend in other archetypal energies. I often start with the hidden one and then add the surface or presenting mode. For example, say a client complains he is "co-dependent." In this case the unintegrated Lover would be presented, meaning the complementary Warrior energies are hidden. It may be helpful for the therapist to sit with the person until she can deeply sense how strong (albeit distorted) the Warrior energies are in that person. For example, the therapist might sense how, against extraordinary odds and with little support, the person has fought fiercely to maintain a commitment to another person. As the therapist feels this, she offers compliments about the person's Warrior energies. The client may find this initially confusing, as she normally doesn't think of herself in this way, but the therapist is quite serious. As the hidden archetype is complimented and elaborated, a trance of absorption often develops in the client. Questions about how this Warrior energy may be helpfully used within the person's life are then developed, and the integration of Warrior/Lover energies is gradually introduced. In this way, a person may be helped to activate the complementary balance of the different archetypal energies, connecting them to self-love and satisfying expressions.

The therapist's use of archetypal energies

We have thus far examined how archetypal energies within the client's experience may be sensed and cultivated for therapeutic purposes. Of course, the same may be said with regard to the therapist. The therapist's presence needs to be filled with the acceptance, empathy, and communion of the Lover; the fierceness, focus, bullshit detector, and challenges of the Warrior; the absorption, enchantment, attention-shifting, and reframing of the Magician/Healer; and the blessings of the King/Queen.

Different therapists may be especially good at one or more of these archetypal skills and energies. Carl Rogers was an archetypal Lover, accepting and communing with whatever the person presented. Albert Ellis is an example of a Warrior therapist, endlessly challenging and confronting the client. Milton Erickson and Carl Whitaker were Magician/Healers, speaking and living from the underworld of the unconscious. Virginia Satir was a Queen therapist, bestowing blessings of personhood on all she met.

Of course, good therapists carry each of the energies to some extent. My mentor, Milton Erickson, was immensely tender and loving, intensely focused and challenging, remarkably enchanting and entrancing, and extraordinarily kingly in his blessings. Each of these energies supported the others, making for an exceptional therapist. I remember sitting in his office when a patient in her late fifties came for her session. She reminded me of June Cleaver, the mother with coifed hair and pearls on the television show, "Leave It to Beaver." Her smile was as big as could be, her charming tone immensely ingratiating. She brought to Erickson the most beautifully wrapped gift I have ever seen, placing it on his desk with a sweet declaration of profound gratitude for all he had done for him. I had seen him accept small gifts from other patients and students, so I couldn't wait for him to open it and see what wonderful gift had been presented.

I was shocked when Erickson looked at her intently, pushed the gift across his desk, and said simply, "I won't accept it."

The woman's smile grew wider, as she insisted, "But you *must* take it, Dr. Erickson."

Erickson pushed the present back again, repeating, "I won't accept it."

Her smile grew still more as she pushed it back. "You *must*, Dr. Erickson."

"I won't accept it."

"You *must!*"

"I won't."

With that he pushed the gift into her lap. She looked down, and he moved from this Warrior mode into more of a Magician-Warrior mode by asking a series of questions about whether she cooked various types of food—Greek, Ethiopian, Thai, and so forth. Each time she said no, and he cheerfully pointed out that his daughter Betty Alice cooked these foods quite well. Finally, tears were welling in her eyes and her head dropped. Erickson then moved into a Lover-Magician mode, asking her softly what her favorite comic strip was. She looked up quizzically, disrupted from her path into withdrawal. He asked her if she had read the Sunday paper Peanuts comic strip, and they began to talk.

It took some years for me to gain any sense of what had happened in the interview. The woman presented with what traditionally might be called a "smiling depression." Her gift was a sort of Trojan horse, a violation of the therapeutic boundaries. Erickson responded with a Warrior's boundary commitment, shifted to the Magician's pattern disruption, and then moved to the soothing healing of the Lover-Magician.

His remarkable facility in shifting among these different modes was, in my view, one of his greatest skills. In our own ways, each of us as therapists is called to cultivate similar skills. The archetype distinctions can be helpful in this regard.

In therapist training groups, one way we examine these distinctions is through a dyadic exercise. A single therapeutic idea—e.g., "you have a inner self"— is selected for communication. Through a group induction, each person is asked to go inside and center. Suggestions for accessing a given archetypal mode are given, especially in terms of posture, images, and feelings. Partners are then asked to keep the felt connection with the archetype as they open their eyes and establish nonverbal connection with each other. Each person is asked to take five minutes to experiment with communicating the given idea from the archetypal mode, especially in terms of touch, rhythm, and tone.

After five minutes, partners are asked to reorient inside and sense their relationship to the archetype—strengths, weaknesses, openings, fears, understandings, and misunderstandings. After taking note of any areas they wish to further examine and develop, they turn their attention to the next archetype and the process repeated. After moving through the four archetypes, the partners make eye connect and feel themselves as the center point for the archetypes. They are asked to imagine the presence of the Lover to their left, the Warrior to their right, the Magician/Healer down below, and the King/Queen above. They are invited to sense a distinct energy emanating from each archetype, flowing through them and intersecting at their somatic center. It is noted that while archetypes are powerful, the person is most important. As they feel each archetype as a distinct resource that guides and helps them, they also feel their own self as they communicate, person to person, the single message ("you really do have an inner self") once again.

This exercise powerfully illustrates the various energies and how they may give different meaning to the same message. It also points out how the therapist might draw on each of the archetypes at different times. This may be especially helpful at those times when the therapist feels stuck in a session. At such times, the therapist may ask which mode she is operating in, and then wonder what it would be like to use a different mode in communicating with the client.

For example, say there's a client whom you dread seeing. You look at your schedule, see who's coming at 11 a.m. and find yourself wondering if it wouldn't be better to quickly develop a headache. Or you find yourself worrying about this person, or being angry about her, or critical of yourself for being a worthless therapist with her. These reactions suggest that, whatever you're doing, perhaps you should do something different.

Using archetypes as a guide, you may ask what mode you're in. Are you trying to help the person through loving acceptance and empathy, only to find yourself overwhelmed and losing boundaries in the process? Are you too fierce, challenging, critical, and cranky with the person, upset because she won't accept your brilliant suggestions? Are you trying to trick, reframe, hypnotize, or otherwise manipulate her?

Whatever the case, take the time first to relax and center, then to move through each archetypal mode. As you move into the Lover mode, ask what needs to be accepted and empathized with in the client's experience, and feel what that would be like to communicate to her. As you move into the Warrior mode, sense what calm centering and focus are needed. Resist the compulsion to try to change things: simply keep appropriate boundaries while not listening too much to the words. (The Warrior doesn't get too caught up in words: she watches and waits patiently.) As you listen from the Magician mode, sense what's not being properly named, where the pull of the underworld is, where the unattended wounds are, what the unconscious of the person is trying to tell you, what a "terrible (but beautiful) gift" the symptom is. And as you enter the King/Queen mode, feel how you have not given blessing or place to some part of the person.

By rotating through each mode, you will find aspects of the person's experience you have overlooked and discover alternate ways of communicating that might be more helpful. In such ways, the archetypes will improve your skills in listening, connecting, and effectively communicating.

Summary

Archetypes are the psychological patterns of human beings that have developed over many generations of living. They represent the challenges and skills each of us faces on our journey to become more of ourselves. Each archetype has many forms and is under the influence of personal, developmental, and social/cultural biases. Consequently, archetypes may support or oppress the experience, vitality, and expressiveness of a person. Psychotherapy is in part an examination of how patterns that oppress may be sponsored and transformed into patterns that support. When we sense and use the archetypal processes flowing through both client and therapist, this task is made much easier.

8

THERAPEUTIC RITUALS

PASSAGES INTO NEW IDENTITIES

> Meditation and ritual have opened for peoples in many cultures the roads between human beings and unnamed and unexplored worlds. The gateways to these realms are guarded by Protectors who test our resolve, our keenness of mind and heart, our friendliness to the unknown. We meet these Protectors in those personal experiences and collective rites that are Threshold experiences, where the husk of alienation is broken down.
>
> The word *threshold* means "the place where things are thrashed or beaten apart." . . . (ritual) is one of the best examples of how the Threshold works to reverse the process of suffering and misfortune into its opposite, to transform an adversary into a Protector.
>
> —*Joan Halifax*, The Fruitful Darkness, *pp. 177–178*

SELF-RELATIONS emphasizes how life flows through the center point of each person, gathering archetypal experiences of the psyche in order to help a person grow and develop greater maturity. It equally emphasizes the skill of mature love, whereby sponsorship of archetypal experience is crucial to discovering and cultivating its human value. We have seen how archetypal experience is especially predominant at times of identity change in a person's life, and how ritual space and method are important during such transformational periods.

This was especially evident to me five years ago, when my father died. Resting and reading in the afternoon, he was felled by a massive heart attack. Upon hearing the news several hours later, I burst into a torrent of tears followed by wave after wave of overwhelming emotions and images. Emotional riptides carried me over great distances, bringing to the surface a multitude of feelings, images, memories and conversations.

Luckily, this journey was navigated within a special context. For three days, family and friends gathered for the ritual process of honoring my dad and saying good-bye to him. With his body as a focal point, ceremonies were performed: a large wake where people gave moving testimonies, a funeral mass, a party, and the burial.

In retrospect, this process was a conversation of the deepest sort, a conversation that midwifed within me (and presumably others) a significant new self-identity. Immersed in the multilevel, multiparticipant, multimodal conversation, yet buoyed by the support of friends and the ritual structures, I found myself saying good-bye to an old self-identity and allowing a new one to be born.

Such crises are inescapable in each of our lives, cutting to the core of our basic identities and demanding the creation of new ones. These crises may be planned or expected—as in a birth or a marriage, a retirement, or a diploma—or they may be quite sudden and shocking—as in a rape, the loss of a child, a brutal assault, or a major illness. Regardless, they all provoke a challenge to redefine one's world in significant ways. When these challenges are successfully navigated, people grow stronger, more confident, and perhaps a bit wiser. Unsuccessful attempts may leave one stranded on an isolated island of despair, subsisting on the bitter fruit of depression, guilt, fear, and shame. Such a diet gives rise to strange and undesirable behaviors, from self-abuse via food, drugs, or sex to self-focus on weaknesses, failures, and doubts. A life of quiet or not so quiet desperation develops, with the greatest passion devoted to self-devaluing acts.

When individuals become mired in these struggles, they sometimes see a therapist in hopes of changing things. Our challenge, of course, is to help them. Our cultural histories are rich with traditions for doing this, for such problems existed (and were solved) long before the advent of modern psychotherapy. This chapter explores how one such tradition, that of healing rituals, may be used in psychotherapy. Some basic distinctions regarding rituals are first outlined. A four-step model for using rituals is then developed. These four steps include (1) suggesting a ritual as a possible solution, (2) planning the ritual, (3) enacting the ritual, and (4) post-ritual activities. A case history illustrates each step.

What are rituals?

Rituals are perhaps the oldest form of therapy.[1] Virtually every culture has developed rituals for major social-psychological functions. Transitional rituals such as baptisms or brisses, weddings, and funerals have been used as bridges from one stage of life into another—at birth, graduations, promotions, rites of passage into adulthood, marriages, retirements, deaths and so on. Continuity rituals such as anniversaries and holidays affirm and regenerate the values and identity of a system. Healing rituals provide recovery from trauma and reincorporation of the dissociated person into the social-psychological community. And atonement rituals provide vehicles for apology and redress of damages done.

In the present view, a ritual is an intense, experiential-archetypal structure that recreates or transforms identity. It is intense in that participants develop heightened absorption that excludes all other frames of reference. It is experiential in that analytic and other processes of the cognitive self are depotentiated, leaving participants deeply immersed in the primary processes of the somatic self, such as bodily feelings, inner imagery, and automatic (spontaneous) process. It is archetypal in that the thoughts, feelings, and behaviors stand for collective, ancestral meanings. (For example, the flag placed on the funeral coffin stands for the deceased's contribution to his or her country; the marriage ring

---

[1] My understanding of rituals has been helped by many authors, especially van der Hart (1983) and Turner (1969). Others include Campbell (1984), Haley (1984), Imber-Black, Roberts, and Whiting (1989), Madanes (1990), and Palazzoli, Boscolo, Cecchin, and Prata (1978). My biggest influence is Milton Erickson (e.g., see Rossi, 1980a, d) and his contributions to working with "the unconscious" with an awareness of social context.

stands for a sacred union.) And lastly, rituals perform meaning at the deeper level of identity: they affirm or transform in a deep cultural language a person's place in a community. In other words, they constitute a meta-conversation between individual(s) and community, between the cognitive self and the somatic self.

Like all archetypal process, rituals are more than ceremonies and distinct from behavioral tasks. A ceremony becomes a ritual only when participants become fully immersed in the nonrational, archaic language of the somatic self; until then, it is merely a traditional behavior sequence having little therapeutic value. (For example, as a child growing up in an Irish Catholic family, I most definitely did not enter a therapeutic ritual space during the nightly ceremony in which the entire family knelt down through five decades of the rosary!)

Similar characteristics separate rituals from behavioral tasks. Rituals involve a predetermined behavioral sequence, such that little cognitive decision-making is needed during its enactment. No meta-commentary by the cognitive self (such as self-talk or evaluations) is permitted, such that no part of the system is split off in an "outside observer" role. This allows holistic properties of the system to be expressed (see Bateson and Bateson, 1987). Special symbols mark ritual space: the place where it occurs, the clothes worn, the words expressed, the behaviors enacted, and the artifacts used all indicate a special, unique situation. Pre- and post-phases are used as inductions into and exits out of ritual space. And binding commitments are secured to promote involvement and heighten the drama and significance of the event.

Rituals occur simultaneously and equally in private and public realities. The inner world is amplified and reorganized, as in a therapeutic trance (Gilligan, 1987). At the same time, outer behaviors signifying crucial relationship changes are performed and witnessed by significant others in the social community. This concurrence of inner and outer changes makes rituals especially powerful and relevant to psychotherapy.

In fact, this feature of rituals is what led me to become interested in them. I had been working a great deal with clients recovering from sexual abuse. The hypnotic experience (with its orientation to "going inside," relaxing and just letting things happen, and "going deeper") proved markedly unsettling to a number of these individuals, especially in its parallels to the traumatic event(s). Cognitive talk also seemed inappropriate, especially in its inability to handle the emotional intensity and dissociational nature of many of the processes. The question thus arose as to what method might make room for what clients were bringing into the conversation, while supporting them in reclaiming their connections to themselves and to the rest of the community. Rituals was one of the emerging answers.

Of course, not all rituals are therapeutic. In fact, many symptoms presented by therapy clients may be expressions of dysfunctional rituals in which individuals recreate a negative self-identity characterized by self-abuse and helplessness. Zoja (1989) lucidly describes how drug addiction is based around ritual process. Also, sexual abuse may be viewed as a traumatic ritual in which a person's biological and psychological boundaries are invaded and desolated. We saw in earlier chapters how this triggers an automatic and immediate "break in belonging" with the rest of the world, engendering a sort of negative trance characterized by hypnotic phenomena such as time distortion, body dissociation, regression, amnesia, and so forth (Gilligan, 1988). This dissociated state can last indefinitely (years and even generations), leading to a "break in relatedness" with the rest of the world and a misidentification of the self as "being" the traumatic event. This misidentification includes the telltale ideas of alienation—for example, "My body is to be abused," "I have no boundaries," "My own needs are nonexistent." When operative, these aliens elicit further self-abusive behaviors (involving food, drugs, relationships, etc.).

A major feature of such patterns is that the communications are primarily at the identity level. That is, they define the self itself rather than pointing to behaviors or actions of the self. Wherever identity is the basic focus of communication, ritual and corresponding altered states of consciousness will come into play.

Viewing such traumatic processes in ritual terms suggests possible therapeutic interventions. Following Erickson's principle of utilization (see Rossi, 1980a, d), the problematic pattern is used as the solution pattern. That is, if a person's problem can be framed in terms of a recurrent ritual, then another ritual may be used as a solution. The remainder of the chapter describes how this might be done via a four-step method.

A *therapy approach to using rituals*

The four steps of the method are listed in Table 8.1. The entire process usually takes four to six weeks, and can be done with individuals, couples, families, or groups. It assumes that certain long-standing, somatically-based complaints may be advantageously described as symptoms of a negative self-identity generated from invasive traumatic experiences. It works to experientially activate and externalize the verbal, visual, and kinesthetic symbols of such "identity events," so that a person may perform a ritual act of casting away the "old identity" and taking on a new one.

The model further assumes that conversations involving "identity shifts" cannot occur primarily within the cognitive self, since such processes generally function to conserve one's existing frame of reference. Thus, the therapist uses hypnotic or similar processes to develop a conversation that utilizes the more experiential-archetypal language of the somatic self. (Use of a more archaic language can be found in many traditional rituals, such as religious ceremonies, theater, or political rallies.) The use of hypnosis occurs within the tradition pioneered by Milton Erickson, featuring a cooperative relationship organized around client values, styles, and resources (see Gilligan, 1987).

TABLE 8.1. FOUR STEPS OF THERAPEUTIC RITUALS

1. Suggest a ritual as a possible solution
2. Planning the ritual
3. Enacting the ritual
4. Reincorporating self into community

Step 1: Frame symptom in ritual terms

The first step is outlined in Table 8.2. The therapist first elicits a description of the symptom the client wishes to change. This description should include both a specific behavioral sequence and any inner experiences occurring during the sequence. For example, Joseph was a 32-year-old computer scientist who sought relief from "an uncontrollable facial grimace" that occurred especially in the presence of his superiors at work. In a typical instance, Joseph would go to present his research at an in-house meeting and find himself tremendously anxious and self-conscious as his face contracted into frightened grimaces when he began his presentation. This usually severely compromised his presentation, to the point where his projects were not being supported and his job advancement retarded. Joseph further reported that he usually sank into the gloom of depression each time the pattern occurred and that depression was experienced by many people in his family.

Joseph was the second of three boys in his family. He described his father as a "brilliant inventor" who was "extremely brutal" with his sons. Joseph emphasized that he had little contact at present with his family (they lived 3,000 miles away) and that he wished to move on with his life without them. He specifically requested hypnosis for symptom relief of his facial grimaces.

The complaint of facial grimaces had several characteristics suggestive of a ritual intervention. Specifically, it was (a) long-

---

TABLE 8.2. SUGGESTING A RITUAL AS A POSSIBLE SOLUTION

1. Identify repetitive symptom, chronic body symptoms, low cognitive insight, nonrational expression.
2. Identify emotional trauma or developmental challenge underlying symptom.
3. Frame symptom positively as incomplete attempt at developmental change or healing process.
4. Elicit full experiential cooperation and motivation to perform ritual.

---

standing, (b) somatically focused, and (c) nonrational and non-cognitively-based. In the domain of hypnosis, which is an intimate cousin to rituals, these are characteristics of trance phenomena. In other words, such symptoms may be viewed as the spontaneous occurrence of a "negative trance," a sort of ritual enactment of some traumatic experience.

Of course, not all such symptoms are best resolved via rituals. Many can be handled by simpler and less time-consuming procedures. (In fact, I usually try such procedures before considering rituals.) To determine the appropriateness of a ritual, a next step is to explore whether the symptom is strongly connected to some emotional trauma or developmental challenge. With Joseph, I initially took his complaint at face value—that is, as simply an undesired behavioral expression that might be modified via some straightforward hypnotic processes. I therefore guided Joseph into a hypnotic trance with a general hypnotic induction centered around suggestions of relaxation and ideomotor finger signaling (Gilligan, 1987). He initially seemed to develop a comfortable trance state, but then suddenly the unexpected occurred. Joseph rapidly dissociated into what appeared a terribly unpleasant state. His body and breathing froze and his face blanched and grimaced. Completely unresponsive to my requests for a verbal report, he seemed to be tailspinning into some otherworldly nightmare. Further suggestions to reorient were also unsuccessful, so I tried to simply join him in his state, saying with soft intensity:

> Joseph, I don't know where you are. Joseph, I don't know why you had to go there . . . but I do know that *you are also here with me.* . . . I do know that *you can hear me and listen to me.* Joseph, I don't know how far away you had to go. . . . I don't know if you need to go even further away in order to comfortably listen to me . . . but I do know you can hear me and respond to me in ways that are appropriate and helpful for you.

Using this sort of talk, I was able to develop a link with Joseph. Over the next ten minutes, I extended this connection to include holding his hand and developing finger signals to communicate with his unconscious mind.

Gradually he reoriented, but upon opening his eyes he froze again in wide-eyed terror, apparently "seeing" someone or something in front of him. On a hunch, I asked if it was his father he saw and his head nodded. Taking hold of his hand and encouraging him to breathe, I gently coached him to expand his attentional field to include me on his right side and to hallucinate a friend on his left side. Gathering strength from these additional relationships, he shouted at his "father" to "get the hell away." The terrifying image receded and Joseph collapsed in a paroxysm of tears.

To reorient him, I walked him around my office for a while. When we sat back down, I sought to ease the seriousness by asking him in a soft humorous tone what he thought of his "standard hypnotic experience." We chuckled a bit, then rode the release to a serious but more relaxed connection. I suggested that perhaps his unconscious mind had decided it was time to say good-bye to some relationship and that this might be the meaning of his recurrent symptom. He seemed intrigued, so we used ideomotor finger signals to ask his unconscious mind (a) whether his symptom of facial grimaces was connected to experiences with his father, (b) whether the dissociational event was connected to some past emotional event with his father, and (c) whether it was time to say good-bye to that abusive relationship.

His yes finger signaled to each of these questions, as it did to the inquiry of whether a specific memory had been accessed. It turned out that the remembered event occurred when Joseph was six years old. He had received a toy train on Christmas morning. Later that day, when he and his brother were playing with it in the basement, Joseph somehow broke the train and its tiny ball bearings scattered across the basement floor. His brother ran and reported the incident to his father, who came roaring down the stairs to unleash a brutal physical assault on Joseph. The boy spent the rest of the day in the basement trying to pick up every last ball bearing while his father periodically returned to beat him again.

This event represented the "neglected self" under the alienating influence of his abusive father. (In rituals, as in hypnosis and any form of artistic expression, it is very important to deal with concrete symbols—that is, specific stories rather than general identities. This event is not seen as the original or singular "cause" of present experience, but rather as a representation of a relationship around which one's identity is organized. Working with more general descriptions such as "the wounded child" or "low self-esteem" does not seem to provide the requisite experiential ground needed for a ritual act to work.)

Joseph was extremely impressed by the responses generated by his unconscious. He voiced an interest in doing something to change his relationship to the memory and inquired about how that might be done. I introduced the possibility of performing a ritual, suggesting that sometimes terribly invasive experiences led people to self-identify with voices, images, and behaviors that really belonged to someone else. It was further noted that such a self-misidentification could give rise to various uncontrollable expressions, such as Joseph's grimacing and depression. Healing rituals were described as processes wherein one first externalized (through letters, paintings, and other experiential processes) these voices, images, and body feelings, then planned and enacted a ritual to once and for all say good-bye to the external influences and hello to one's own voice, images, and feelings. A few simple examples were offered to emphasize how rituals were co-created by therapist and client, with the therapist providing expertise on structures and the client generating the specific materials, making the decisions and enacting the ritual.

It was also noted that individuals really needed to sense that the time was right to do the ritual, for it required their full commitment and participation. To stress this point, Joseph was asked to take the next week to decide whether to commit to such a process. He returned the following week and said he was definitely interested in doing the ritual. (If a full commitment is not possible, the therapist should abandon the possibility of a ritual and explore other interventions.)

The above description indicates the importance of connecting the complaint to an emotional trauma or developmental challenge, framing the symptom as an incomplete or unsuccessful attempt to change one's identity in relation to the event or challenge, and then suggesting therapeutic rituals as an effective means for transforming one's identity and dissolving the symptom. The success of the ritual requires the client's full motivation and participation.

The case also illustrates how the connection of the symptom with a trauma must occur experientially. An intellectual hypothesis that symptom X is connected to event Y is wholly inadequate, for it leaves the therapeutic conversation at a cognitive level. (To reiterate, it is precisely in those cases where cognitive understanding is of little or no value that rituals may be especially indicated.) The language of ritual connects more with the somatic self, much as symptoms and hypnotic phenomena do (Gilligan, 1988). Thus, the therapist should make use of such language to lead into the possibility of a ritual.

There are, of course, other methods for conducting this experiential inquiry. With some clients I suggest that they develop a light "centering" trance, contemplate the question, "What is this (symptomatic) experience connected to?" and then use crayons or paints on art paper to let their "unconscious mind" express a response. This can be done in the office with the therapist or at home during the week. In the latter case, therapists should ensure that clients have adequate resources—for example, the presence of a friend or a physical symbol (see Dolan, 1991)—to stay centered if the process recalls difficult material.

Another possibility is to use other hypnotic explorations—for example, general "searches" for relevant material (Gilligan, 1987; Lankton & Lankton, 1983) or ideomotor questions. Whatever the method used, the therapist seeks to frame a chronic symptom over which the client feels no control as an "identity event" that may be transformed via ritual.

Step 2: Planning the ritual

This second step typically takes three to six weeks. As Table 8.3 indicates, it involves generating and externalizing the experiential symbols of both the old and new selves and then evolving a ritual that allows the transition from the former to the latter. Time and care are taken to ensure that this process is generated, guided, and ratified each step of the way by the client's somatic self ("the unconscious") rather than his cognitive self.

The first two parts of the planning are usually done concur-

TABLE 8.3. PLANNING THE RITUAL

1. Have client develop physical symbols of old identity.
2. Have client develop physical symbols of new identity.
3. Identify basic ritual act (burning, burying, declarations, etc.).
4. Plan actual ritual (where, with whom, when, what specific actions).
5. Have client emotionally/spiritually prepare for ritual.

---

rently. First, the verbal conversations that the person has internalized are experientially activated and externalized in physical form. This is often done via letter writing. In the case of Joseph, I suggested (and he ratified via finger signals) that he take forty minutes each day to write two letters. Following the more structured approaches inherent in ritual, we decided upon a specific time of day (8 p.m.) and place (his study) to write these letters. After a brief centering process, he would spend twenty minutes writing a first letter to someone involved in the "old self" event of the broken train. On different nights, this person was (six-year-old) Joseph, his brother, his father, and his mother. The letter was to describe what happened, how he felt then, how the event had influenced his subsequent self-image, and what he wanted to do about it now. The second letter (also written in twenty minutes) was to his "future self" and specified the life he was interested in living and differences in his behavior. (Sometimes a person finds it more helpful to write this letter from his future self back to his present self or to a younger, childhood self.)

Before this task is carried out, hypnotic questioning is used to ensure that it is appropriate and that sufficient resources are available. Often, some modifications are needed. For example, a person or another resource may need to be present with the client while he writes a letter (Dolan, 1991). Hypnotic questioning is also used in the next session to determine whether any more letters need to be written. The therapist might read the letters to ensure the client is centered and connected to the process. (For example, I discontinued the ritual process with a client who wrote letters to his younger self in a nasty, caustic manner, sensing that it was premature to develop a healing ritual.) Each of these ongoing "checks" indicates how the ritual planning is shaped and modified by an ongoing collaborative process between therapist and client(s).

The next externalization process involves images. As in the letter writing, it is suggested that the client take forty minutes daily (over a week or so) to paint, draw (with color), collage, or otherwise visually display first the "old self" event and then some version of the "new self." Clients concerned about having no artistic talent ("I can't draw") are encouraged to just let happen whatever happens, from actual depictions to just intense colors. They are encouraged to let these expressions come from their own inner selves while focusing on the questions, "What did the traumatic event look or feel like?" (for the first drawing) and "What will things look or feel like after the symptom (or problem) is resolved?" Again, the therapist takes steps to check (a) that the process is appropriate, (b) that sufficient processes are available, (c) that the person is emotionally connected and centered in the process, and (d) whether any further work needs to be done after the person returns in the next session with the externalized images.

The client is then asked during the following week to select physical symbols of the new and old selves. Self-hypnosis, meditation, and open curiosity might be used in this regard. The person need not cognitively understand or explain why he selected a symbol. Examples of "old self" symbols include the baby clothes knitted by a woman who had lost her baby daughter, the photograph a woman found of the uncle who sexually molested her, and the toy train (resembling the old train) that Joseph bought. Examples of the "new self" symbols include Japanese bonsai trees purchased by the woman grieving her daughter, African shields and spears chosen by the sexually abused woman, and a ring by Joseph. Again, the therapist works to ensure that each of these selections is appropriate and complete.

The client has now concretized and externalized symbols of the old and new self. The next step is to select the basic ritual acts for saying good-bye to the old self and welcoming the new self. The therapist might outline "menu selections"—for example, burning or burying the "old self" materials—and then support clients in making their own choices. Hypnosis helped Joseph to generate the ritual acts of (a) dumping ball bearings of a toy train over actual train tracks and then (b) crossing the tracks to "the other side" to declare his new self. These choices were ratified by his ideomotor finger signals.

The next session involves planning the details of where, when, how, and with whom the ritual will occur. Each should be considered carefully, and all discussions should be ratified in some significant way by the person. With Joseph, the plan was to go to the train tracks a mile or so from my office. He would bring the train along with the letters and drawings. The "saying good-bye" part of the ritual would involve reading aloud the "old self" letters and showing the pictures before dumping the toy train's ball bearings over the train tracks as a way of declaring his letting go of these symbols. He would then cross the tracks and do several ceremonial declarations of the new self.

The issue of who else to include is especially important, since a ritual takes place at the intersection between two worlds: the public and private, or the inner and outer. Persons performing a ritual act are not only reorganizing their inner world, but also declaring to others a new social self. Witnesses both observe a person's declarations and participate in and validate the creation of a new social and psychological identity. This extraordinary complementarity is a major reason for the effectiveness of healing rituals.

With Joseph, this issue proved to be painful. After much deliberation he decided that he didn't feel sufficiently close to anyone to invite someone to participate. (Developing friendships and community became a major focus of his post-ritual activities.) He asked me to participate, and I reiterated that I would, though primarily in the role of the "ritual specialist" guiding the process and providing minimal coaching if needed. He also accepted my suggestion that he consider communicating the effects of the ritual to family members (all of whom lived 3,000 miles away).

As a last preparation step, the client is asked to take the week before the ritual to orient inwardly and emotionally prepare for the event. Depending on a person's practices and values, this might include solitary walks, diary writing, self-hypnosis or meditation, light fasting, or prayer. This is a crucial step in most traditional rituals (as well as other important performances), since it shifts attention away from "business as usual" toward a dramatically heightened inner focus.

Step 3: Enacting the ritual

The performance of the ritual has three parts: the pre-ritual induction that develops the liminal consciousness of ritual space (Turner, 1969); the ritual itself; and the post-ritual process that incorporates a person back into the normal social space. The pre-ritual induction is similar to a hypnotic induction, involving the use of attentional narrowing, repetition and rhythm, and symbolic activities that shift the person into a heightened state of archetypal-somatic absorption (Gilligan, 1987). This may involve convocational speeches, chants, prayers, inward meditations, poems, or other ceremonial acts. The induced mood is generally serious and intense, with a sense that something very important is about to happen.

In the case of Joseph, he arrived at my office on the appointed day, bringing with him his ritual symbols: the letters, drawings, and train. In a soft and focused conversation we reviewed all that had happened over the past month and he reaffirmed his commitment to performing the ritual. We drove in separate cars to the ritual site (the railroad crossroads), got out, and marked out the ritual space with rocks and sticks. Joseph faced the tracks, laid out the ritual symbols of the old self, oriented inwardly for several minutes, then turned to me and indicated his readiness.

When I nodded solemnly for him to "go for it," he again closed his eyes to deepen his involvement. When he opened them several minutes later, he appeared intensely focused and in an emotionally heightened, altered state of consciousness. Fighting back tears, he visualized all around him the members of his family. His strong, vulnerable voice cracked with emotion as he greeted each person and declared his purpose in summoning them to the event. He picked up the "old self" letters and read them one by one, declaring after each that he was finished with those words and then proceeded to tear up the letter. His emotions appeared ready to overwhelm him periodically but each time he paused to compose and center himself before continuing. (Some clients may benefit from some gentle support and encouragement during such times.)

He next displayed each "old self" drawing, describing what had happened, how he felt then, how his identity had been influenced, and how he was ready now to let go of this self-image. He then ripped up the images and placed the torn tatters into a box, which was later burned. Waves of emotions—grief, anger, sadness—surged through him during this process.

The final "good-bye" process involved the toy train. He had removed its bottom to expose the ball bearings, which were now held in place by a single piece of tape. As he focused his attention on the train in his hand, he lapsed into convulsive sobs. After a minute or so, I moved in, whispered for him to breathe and allow the feelings to just "move through," and gently encouraged him to continue. This helped him to center and refocus his attention on the ritual task. Looking at his imagined family, he declared that the time had come for him to move on. He recounted the "train incident" in slow, measured tones, then announced that he was ready to reclaim that event for his own development. In ceremonial declaration he held the toy train over the train tracks, removed the tape, and let the ball bearings pour out all over the tracks. (I had not appreciated until then how small these ball bearings were, or how many of them there were.) Many emotions were also released, but Joseph seemed to grow in strength and stature as they did. Finally he turned to me and said he was ready to "move on."

With Joseph in the lead, we walked over the crossroads. He then performed the "new self" ritual by reading the letters written to his future self, showing the drawings, and ceremoniously donning the ring he had selected to symbolize his new commitment. This part of the ritual seemed much easier for him, as if he was guided by some newfound strength and spirit.

One final piece of the ritual remained. Joseph had decided during self-hypnotic explorations several weeks earlier to send the toy train back east to his brother (who had "turned him in"), along with a letter. In this poignant letter, Joseph mentioned the horrible childhood they had shared, and how it apparently made both of them depressed and unhappy during their adult lives. (His brother struggled with chronic depression.) Joseph expressed his commitment to free himself from such unhappiness and then recounted the train incident from childhood. He described the ritual process in which he had been immersed over the previous six weeks and noted that during his self-explorations he had developed the strong sense that he should send the train to his brother after the ritual, since he was now finished with it. He confessed that he was not entirely sure why this was important or what his brother should do with it (he suggested donating it to charity), but felt strongly that he was finished with it and that it should be given to his brother. (At several points during the weeks of ritual preparation, Joseph confirmed to me through ideomotor signaling that this was indeed a proper course of action.) He concluded the letter by stating that he loved his brother deeply and wanted their relationship to deepen and grow stronger.

Joseph placed this letter along with the train in a package he had addressed to his brother. We drove in our respective cars to the post office, and he went in and mailed it. Upon returning he reported that during the ritual an incredible weight that "had been there for so long I was no longer aware it was there" had lifted and dissolved. He looked and sounded remarkably calm, centered, and confident. I complimented him on the incredible courage and commitment he had shown during the ritual (and throughout the entire preparation process) and told him he had done a great job.

He had arranged (at my suggestion) to take the rest of the day off, so I encouraged him to go home to relax and savor his achievements. I also suggested that he use letter writing anytime over the next couple of weeks that he felt any "old voices" revisiting him, since it was a good way to externalize and let go of occasional residual processes that were "looking to leave and go back to where they belong." (Many clients find this process very helpful.) I also reminded him he could review any of the "new self" letters, images, or symbols that he was taking home with him, especially anytime he needed to center himself.

Step 4: Reincorporating self into community

Planning and performing a therapeutic ritual is an especially intense process. Participants withdraw from everyday life—emotionally, psychologically and behaviorally—for a prolonged time and become deeply immersed in alternate, inner realities. It is therefore crucial that the person be reincorporated back into the social community following a ritual. Any further "inner work" explorations are generally curtailed and attention oriented to practical challenges and responsibilities, such as friends, jobs, families, and social skills. Therapy ends after another session or two, unless short-term concrete goals are negotiated. Rituals generally work as an "all or none" process, with transformation occurring during the ritual act itself. Thus, additional inner work on the issue is often counterproductive.

When Joseph returned the following week, he looked great. He said that after the ritual he celebrated by going shopping for a new wardrobe. He felt alive and "open," and proudly reported making a presentation at work without any grimaces. (He reported feeling very aware of the new ring on his finger during the presentation.) He felt confident about continuing these new behaviors and we mutually agreed that, since the therapeutic goals had been achieved, we could stop meeting.

About a year later, Joseph called me on the phone. He reported a continuing absence of facial grimaces and requested some hypnosis to help him in his new hobby of kick-boxing. We spent several sessions on this project, during which time he reported having a great time at his job.

Summary

The case of Joseph illustrates how rituals may be powerful mediums for therapeutic change. They allow the transformation of identity and the dissolution of undesired symptoms. Rituals are decidedly nonrational, archetypal events in which individuals tap into deep inner resources and engage in profound experiential-symbolic conversations. Most important, they empower individuals to externalize alien images, voices, and behaviors and rediscover and claim their own voices, visions, and bodies.

While the case example involved an individual, rituals may also be used with couples, families, and groups. They may be helpful with many different types of complaints. I have used rituals with individuals, couples, or families dealing with sexual abuse (e.g., incest or rape), and also with groups of incest survivors. Divorce ceremonies (with one or both people) including friends and family can be helpful. Purification and atonement rituals may work in cases of infidelity. Rituals marking deaths (including abortions) have been profoundly moving. Other rituals may be co-created for rites of passage, eating disorders, substance abuse, and leaving abusive communities (e.g., cults, ritual abuse).

In each of these cases, the therapist respects and empowers the inner uniqueness and intelligence of clients so that the actual symbols and acts of the ritual emanate from them, not from the therapist. The therapist acts as a "ritual specialist" who provides possible structures, supports clients in staying in relationship with their archetypal-somatic processes, and witnesses and occasionally guides the process. When clients and therapists are both fully participating and contributing, each in their own way, the ritual can indeed be a therapeutic event.

In terms of self-relations, rituals reconnect the somatic self and the cognitive self, thereby giving birth to a new experience of the relational self. It assumes that some event has severed the connection between the two selves, so that the somatic self is operating without sponsorship from the cognitive self. The symptom is an attempt by the somatic self to integrate certain experiences and understandings into the relational self. Rituals are complex acts of sponsorship that provide place for the symptom to be converted into a solution.

EPILOGUE

The deep parts of my life pour onward,
as if the river shores were opening out.
It seems that things are more like me now,
that I can see farther into paintings.
I feel closer to what language cannot reach.

—*Ranier Rilke, "Moving Forward"*

WE HAVE EXAMINED the basic idea of a relational self, both in terms of a connection between mind and nature, as well as self and other, and in terms of a felt field from which all dualities arise and return. We have seen how this generative self is known through a center of consciousness in the somatic self, a psychological relationship of "I and thou" in the cognitive self, and a field of awareness in the relational self. Sustained breaks in knowing any of these levels create significant problems. Psychotherapy is one of the major contemporary ritual methods for healing these breaks and supporting growth and development.

We have seen how the important presence in all of this is love. We have asked whether people like Christ, Nelson Mandela, Mother Theresa, Gandhi, and Milton Erickson were simply nice people who emphasized love and acceptance, or whether they were something much more: courageous individuals who practiced and made visible a power of love far greater than physical force or violence. In accepting the latter view, we reject "ghettoized" versions of love as a weak, sentimental, dangerous, unethical, or irrelevant emotion. We accept and seek to realize an understanding of love as a rigorous practice, a mature skill, a courage, a spirit, a discipline, and the basis for all healing. Because it does not depend on conditions or circumstance, it may be experienced and used by anyone, any time, any place.

The dominant principle underlying effective love is mature sponsorship. We have seen that just as any decent parent would emphasize the skill of love as the basis for effective parenting, therapists may acknowledge love and its corresponding principle of sponsorship as the basis for effective therapy. An effective sponsor (1) awakens you to the goodness and intelligence of your own being, (2) awakens you to the goodness and intelligence in the world all around you, and (3) introduces you to some practices and traditions for developing a relational self that connects self-in-world and world-in-self. In other words, sponsors encourage devotion to self-realization, service and contribution to the world, and appreciation of the integral relationship between the two.

Sponsors appreciate that the river of life runs through everything and everybody, bringing those experiences needed for growth and development. They know that mature human presence and attentiveness are required to realize the human value and forms of these basic life energies, and seek to pass on this realization and its corresponding skills and traditions to others. As any parent will attest, how this is effectively done is forever changing. Just when you think you've got it figured out, the rug is pulled from under you once again.

Thus, the suggestions made in the previous pages are not meant as overarching truth or unchanging method. They are offered as poems, prayers, and promises. They are intended as words of encouragement to develop the disciplined listening, effective suffering, joyful acceptance, vulnerable receptivity, rigorous flexibility, courageous speaking, transformative relating, and humble surrender needed to practice effective love.

Since love is the basis for all creative action, it touches on every important area of human being and becoming. In this regard, we have only addressed a few small areas. Our bias has been toward the psychological and spiritual aspects of the relational self, especially as it applies to individuals. The omissions are significant. For example, much attention is needed to repair and practice the relational self at the larger social levels of community. Thus, I hope this book is taken as a beginning and that kindred spirits will expand and extend its scope.

In doing so, we move closer to realizing the omega point of Teilhard de Chardin (in Sell, 1995, p. vi):

> The day will come when, after harnessing the winds, the tides, and gravitation, we shall harness for God the energies of love. And on that day, for the second time in the history of the world, man will have discovered fire.

To move toward that day, we are encouraged by Krishnamurti's (1967, p. 73) sage advice:

> Put away the book, the description, the tradition, the authority, and take the journey of self-discovery. Love, and don't be caught in opinions and ideas about love is or should be. When you love, everything will come right. Love has its own action. Love, and you will know the blessings of it. Keep away from the authority who tells you what love is and what it is not. No authority knows and he who knows cannot tell. Love, and there is understanding.

May the force be with you.

REFERENCES

Barks, C. (Ed. & Trans.). (1995). *The essential Rumi*. New York: Harper Collins.

Bateson, G. (1955/1972). A theory of play and fantasy: A report on theoretical aspects of the project for study of the role of paradoxes of abstraction in communication. In G. Bateson, *Steps to an ecology of mind*. New York: Ballantine.

Bateson, G. (1970/1972). Form, substance and difference. Reprinted in G. Bateson, *Steps to an ecology of mind*. New York: Ballantine.

Bateson, G. (1972). *Steps to an ecology of mind*. New York: Ballantine.

Bateson, G. (1975). Ecology of mind: The sacred. In R. Fields (Ed.), *Loka: A Journal from the Naropa Institute*. Garden City: Anchor.

Bateson, G. (1979). *Mind and nature: A necessary unity*. New York: Dutton.

Bateson, G., & Bateson, M. C. (1987). *Angels fear: Towards an epistemology of the sacred*. New York: Macmillan.

Baudrillard, J. (1995). The map precedes the territory. In W. T. Anderson (Ed.), *The truth about truth: De-confusing and re-constructing the postmodern world*. New York: G. P. Putnam's Sons

Berry, W. (1977). *The unsettling of America: Culture and agriculture*. San Francisco: Sierra Club.

Blakeslee, S. (Jan. 23,1996). Complex and hidden brain in the stomach makes butterflies and stomach aches. *New York Times*.

Bly, R. (1986). The good silence. In R. Bly, *Selected poems*. New York: Harper & Row.

Bly, R. (1986). Four ways of knowledge. In R. Bly, *Selected poems*. New York: Harper & Row.

Buber, M. (1923/1958). *I and thou*. (R. G. Smith, Trans.). New York: Scribner & Sons.

Buber, M. (1947). *Tales of the Hassidism*. New York: Schocken Books.

Campbell, J. (1984). *The way of the animal powers*. London: Times Books.

Capek, M. (1961). *The philosophical impact of contemporary physics*. Princeton, NJ: D. Van Nostrand.

Carolan, T. (May, 1996). The wild mind of Gary Snyder. *Shambhala Sun*.

Castenada, C. (1974). *Tales of power*. New York: Simon & Schuster.

Chodron, P. (1994). *Start where you are: A guide to compassionate living*. Boston: Shambhala.

Chopra, D. (1989). *Quantum healing: Exploring the frontiers of mind/body medicine*. New York: Bantam.

Csikszentmihalyi, M. (1990). *Flow: The psychology of optimal experience*. New York: Harper Perennial.

Deikman, A. (1963). Experimental meditation. *Journal of Nervous and Mental Disorders, 135*, 329–373.

Deikman, A. (1966). Deautomization and the mystic experience. *Psychiatry, 29*, 324–388.

Deng, Ming-Dao (1992). *365 Tao*. New York: Harper Collins.

Derrida, J. (1977). *Of grammatology*. Baltimore: Johns Hopkins University Press.

de Shazer, S. (1985). *Keys to solution in brief therapy*. New York: Norton.

Dolan, Y. (1991). *Resolving sexual abuse: Solution-focused therapy and Ericksonian hypnosis for adult survivors*. New York: Norton.

Eliot, T. S. (1963). The four quartets. In T. S. Eliot, *Collected poems: 1909–1962*. San Diego: Harcourt Brace Jovanovich.

Epstein, S. (1994). Integration of the cognitive and the psychodynamic unconscious. *American Psychologist, 49, 8*, 709–724.

Erickson, M. H. (1962/1980b) Basic psychological problems in hypnotic research. In G. Estrabrooks (Ed.), *Hypnosis: Current problems*. New York: Harper & Row. Reprinted in E. L. Rossi (Ed.), *The collected papers of Milton H. Erickson on hypnosis* (Vol. 2). New York: Irvington.

Erickson, M. H. & Kubie, L. (1940/1980d). The translation of the cryptic automatic writing of one hypnotic subject by another in a trancelike dissociated state. *Psychoanalytic Quarterly, 10*(1), 5–63. Reprinted in E. L. Rossi (Ed.) *The collected papers of Milton H. Erickson on hypnosis* (Vol. 4). New York: Irvington.

Erickson, M. H., & Rossi, E. L. (1979). *Hypnotherapy: An exploratory casebook*. New York: Irvington.

Erlich, D. (July, 1996). Meredith Monk: In search of the primordial voice. *Shambhala Sun*.

Fields, R. (1991). *The code of the warrior: In history, myth, and everyday life*. New York: Harper Perennial.

Flemons, D. (1991). *Completing distinctions: Interweaving the ideas of Gregory Bateson and Taoism into a unique approach to therapy*. Boston: Shambhala.

Forster, E. M. (1985). *Howard's end*. New York: Bantam.

Freud, S. (1909). Analysis of a phobia in a five-year-old boy. In J. Strachey (Ed. & Trans.), *The standard edition of the complete psychological works of Sigmund Freud* (Vol. 10, pp. 3–152). New York: Norton.

Freud, S. (1912). Recommendations to physicians practicing psychoanalysis. In J. Strachey (Ed. & Trans.), *The standard edition of the complete psychological works of Sigmund Freud* (Vol. 18, pp. 234–254). New York: Norton.

Fromm, E. (1947). *Man for himself: An inquiry into the psychology of ethics.* New York: Holt, Rhinehart, & Winston.

Fromm, E. (1956). *The art of loving.* New York: Harper & Row.

Gendlin, E. (1978). *Focusing.* New York: Bantam.

Gershon, M. D., Kirchgessner, A. L., & Wade, P. (1994). Functional autonomy of the enteric nervous system. In L. R. Johnson (Ed.), *Physiology of the gastrointestinal tract, Third ed.* New York: Raven.

Gibran, K. (1923). *The prophet.* New York: Knopf.

Gilligan, S. G. (1987). *Therapeutic trances: The cooperation principle in Ericksonian hypnotherapy.* New York: Brunner/Mazel.

Gilligan, S. G. (1988). Symptom phenomena as trance phenomena. In J. Zeig & S. Lankton (Eds.), *Developing Ericksonian therapy: State of the art.* New York: Brunner/Mazel.

Gilligan, S. G. (1994). The fight against fundamentalism: Searching for soul in Erickson's legacy. In J. Zeig (Ed.), *Ericksonian methods: The essence of the story.* New York: Brunner/Mazel.

Gilligan, S. G. (1996). The relational self: The expanding of love beyond desire. In M. Hoyt (Ed.), *Constructive therapies: Expanding and integrating effective* (Vol. 2). New York: Guilford.

Gilligan, S. G. & Bower, G. H. (1984). Cognitive consequences of emotional arousal. In C. E. Izard, J. Kagan, & R. Zajonc (Eds.), *Emotions, cognitions, and behavior.* New York: Cambridge Press.

Gilligan, S. G. & Price, R. (Eds.). (1993). *Therapeutic conversations.* New York: Norton.

Ginsberg, A. (1992). Meditation and poetics. In J. Welwood (Ed.), *Everyday life as spiritual path.* Boston: Shambhala.

Haley, J. (1984). *Ordeal therapy.* San Francisco: Jossey-Bass.

Halifax, J. (1994). *The fruitful darkness: Reconnecting with the body of the earth.* New York: Harper Collins Paperback.

Herman, J. (1992). *Trauma and recovery: The aftermath of violence from domestic abuse to political terror.* New York: Basic.

Houston, J. (1980). *Life force: The psycho-historical recovery of the Self.* New York: Dell.

Houston, J. (1987). *The search for the beloved: Journeys in mythology and sacred psychology.* Los Angeles: Tarcher.

Imber-Black, E., Roberts, J., & Whiting, R. (1989). *Rituals in families and family therapy.* New York: Norton.

Jeffares, A. N. (Ed.). (1974). *W. B. Yeats: Selected poetry.* London: Pan.

Jenkins, A. (1990). *Invitations to responsibility: The therapeutic engagement of men who are violent and abusive.* Adelaide, South Australia: Dulwich Centre Publications.

Joyce, J. (1916). *A portrait of an artist as a young man.* London: Jonathan Cape, Ltd.

Jung, C. G. (1916/1971). *The structure and dynamics of the psyche.* Reprinted in J. Campbell (Ed.), *The portable Jung.* New York: Penguin.

Jung, C. G. (1919/1971). Instinct and the unconscious. Reprinted in J. Campbell (Ed.), *The portable Jung.* New York: Penguin.

Jung, C. G. (1954). *Symbols of transformation.* Princeton, NJ: Princeton University Press.

Jung. C. G. (1957). Commentary on "The secret of the golden flower". In H. Read, M. Fordham, & G. Adler (Eds.) and R. F. C. Hull (Trans.), *The collected works of C. G. Jung* (Vol. 13). Princeton, NJ: Princeton University Press.

Jung, C. G. (1969). *The psychology of the transference.* Princeton, NJ: Princeton University Press.

Keen, S. (1986). *Faces of the enemy: Reflections of the hostile imagination.* San Francisco: Harper & Row.

Keeney, B. (1977). *On paradigmatic change: Conversations with Gregory Bateson.* Unpublished manuscript.

Keeney, B. (1983). *Aesthetics of change.* New York: Guilford.

Keller, H. (1902/1988). *The story of my life.* New York: Signet.

Koestler, A. (1964). *The act of creation: A study of the conscious and unconscious in science and art.* New York: Dell.

Krishnamurti, J. (1967). *Commentaries on living: Third series.* Wheaton, IL: Theosophical Publishing House.

Laing, R. D. (1987). Hatred of health. *Journal of contemplative psychotherapy, 4.*

Lankton, S., & Lankton, C. (1983). *The answer within: A framework for Ericksonian hypnotherapy.* New York: Brunner/Mazel.

Machado, A. (1983). *Times alone: Selected poems of Antonio Machado* (R. Bly, Trans.). Middletown, CT: Wesleyan University Press.

Madanes, C. (1990). *Sex, love, and violence: Strategies for transformation.* New York: Norton.

Merton. T. (1948). *The seven storey mountain.* New York: Harcourt Brace.

Merton, T. (1964). (Ed.). *Gandhi on non-violence: A selection from the writings of Mahatma Gandhi.* New York: New Directions.

Moore, R. & Gillette, D. (1990). *King, warrior, magician, lover: Rediscovering the archetypes of the mature masculine.* New York: Harper Collins.

Neruda, P. (1969). Keeping quiet. In *Extravagaria* (A. Reid, Trans.). London: Farrar, Straus & Giroux.

Nhat Hanh, T. (1975). *The miracle of mindfulness.* Boston: Beacon.

Nhat Hanh, T. (1991). *Peace is every step: The path of mindfulness in everyday life.* New York: Bantam.

O'Hara, M. (1996). *Relational empathy: From modernist egocentrism to postmodern contextualism.* Manuscript in preparation.

Osbon, D. (1991). (Ed.) *Reflections on the art of living: A Joseph Campbell Companion.* New York: HarperCollins.

Oz, A. (1995). Like a gangster on the night of the long knives. In N. de Lange (Trans.), *Under this blazing light.* Cambridge: Cambridge University Press.

Palazzoli, M. S., Boscolo, L., Cecchin, G. F., & Prata, G. (1978). *Paradox and counterparadox.* New York: Jason Aaronson.

Pearson, C. S. (1989). *The hero within: Six archetypes we live by*. New York: Harper & Row.

Richards, M. C. (1962). *Centering: In pottery, poetry and the person*. Middletown, CT: Wesleyan U. Press.

Rilke, R. (1981a). Moving forward. In R. Bly (Ed. & Trans.), *Selected poems of Rainier Maria Rilke*. New York: Harper & Row.

Rilke, R. (1981b). The man watching. In R. Bly (Ed. & Trans.), *Selected poems of Rainier Maria Rilke*. New York: Harper & Row.

Rossi, E. L. (1977). The cerebral hemispheres in analytical psychology. *Journal of analytical psychology*, 22, 32–51.

Rossi, E. L. (1980a). (Ed.). *The collected papers of Milton H. Erickson on hypnosis* (Vol. 1). New York: Irvington.

Rossi, E. L. (1980b). (Ed.). *The collected papers of Milton H. Erickson on hypnosis* (Vol. 2). New York: Irvington.

Rossi, E. L. (1980c). (Ed.). *The collected papers of Milton H. Erickson on hypnosis* (Vol. 3). New York: Irvington.

Rossi, E. L. (1980d). (Ed.). *The collected papers of Milton H. Erickson on hypnosis* (Vol. 4). New York: Irvington.

Schiller, D. (1994). *The little Zen companion*. New York: Workman.

Sell, E. H. (1995). (Ed.). *The spirit of loving: Reflections on love and relationship by writers, psychotherapists, and spiritual teachers*. Boston: Shambhala.

Selye, H. (1956). *The stress of life*. New York: McGraw-Hill.

Shapiro, F. (1995). *Eye movement desensitization and reprocessing*. New York: Guilford.

Sharansky, N. (1988). *Fear no evil* (S. Hoffman, Trans.). New York: Random House.

Sivaraska, S., & Harding, V. (1995). Loving the enemy. *Shambhala Sun*, 4(2), 61–63.

Snyder, G. (1980). *The real work: Interviews & talks, 1964–1979*. Edited by William Scott McLean. New York: New Directions.

Some, M. (1994). *Of water and spirit: Ritual, magic, and initiation in the life of an African Shaman*. New York: Tarcher.

Stephens, J. (Ed.). (1992). *The art of peace: Teachings of the founder of aikido*. Boston: Shambhala.

Strozier, C. (1994). *Apocalypse: The psychology of fundamentalism in America*. New York: Beacon.

Suzuki, D. T. (1960). Lectures on Zen Buddhism. In E. Fromm, D. T. Suzuki, & R. DeMartino (Eds.), *Zen Buddhism and psychoanalysis*. New York: Harper Colophon.

Tart, C. (Ed.). (1969). *Altered states of consciousness*. Garden City, NY: Doubleday.

Tohei, K. (1976). *Book of Ki: Co-ordinating mind and body in daily life*. Tokyo: Japan Publications.

Toms, M. (1994). Writing from the belly: An interview with Isabel Allende. *Common Boundary*, 12(3), 16–23.

Trungpa, C. (1984). *Shambhala: The sacred path of the warrior*. Boston: Shambhala.

Trungpa, C. (1993). *Training the mind and cultivating loving-kindness.* Boston: Shambhala.

Turner, V. (1969). *The ritual process: Structure and anti-structure.* Chicago: Aldine.

van der Hart, O. (1983). *Rituals in psychotherapy: Transition and continuity.* New York: Irvington.

van der Kolk, B. (1994). The body keeps the score: Memory and the evolving psychobiology of posttraumatic stress. *Harvard Rev. Psychiatry, 1,* 253–265.

Varela, F. J., Thompson, E., & Rosch, E. (1993). *The embodied mind: Cognitive science and human experience.* Cambridge, MA: MIT Press.

Watzlawick, P., Weakland, J., & Fisch, R. (1974). *Change: Principles of problem formation and problem resolution.* New York: Norton.

White, M., & Epston, D. (1990). *Narrative means to therapeutic ends.* New York: Norton.

Wilber, K. (1995). *Sex, ecology, spirituality.* Boston: Shambhala.

Wilson, B. (1967). *As Bill sees it: The AA way of life.* New York: Alcoholics Anonymous World Services Inc.

Wittgentstein, L. (1951). *Tractatus logico-philosophicus.* New York: Humanities Press.

Woodman, M. (1993). *Conscious femininity: Interviews with Marion Woodman.* Toronto: Inner City Books.

Yeats, W. B. (Ed.). (1905/1979). *The poems of William Blake.* London: Routledge & Kegan Paul.

Zeig, J. K. (1980). *A teaching seminar with Milton Erickson.* New York: Brunner/Mazel.

Zoja, L. (1989). *Drugs, addiction, and initiation: The modern search for ritual.* Boston, MA: Sigo.

Index

orientation to complementary identities, 112–14
in relational cycles, 46–47
relational entrainment, 91–92
remembering experiences of self-transcendence, 92
to restore break in cognitive-somatic relatedness, 94–95
in self-love, 87–88
significance of, xvi
three-point attention, 90–91
for tonglen approach, 120–21
vertical centering, 85–86
Auden, W. H., 3

Bateson, G., 22, 35n, 39–40, 44–45, 46, 60–61, 73, 74, 180
Bateson, M. C., 180
Baudrillard, J., 39
beingness, 49, 50–54, 69
belly centering, 84–85
belongingness, 49, 54–60, 69, 129
Berry, Wendell, 8, 127
Blake, William, 35
Blakeslee, S., 84
blessings, 53, 54
for expression of archetype, 161
Bly, R., 41, 118
Blyth, R. H., 54
Bohr, Neils, 41
Boscolo, L., 179n
Bower, G. H., 145
breathing awareness, 75–76
Buber, M., 62

Campbell, J., 22, 24–25, 55, 179n
Capek, M., 55
Carolan, T., 43
Castaneda, C., 90
Cecchin, G. F., 179n
centering, 6–7
agency of mindfulness for, 11
belly, 84–85
clinical application, 86–88
clinical techniques, 80–81
connecting multiple centers, 85–86
goals, 10, 21
grounding exercises, 88–89
heart, 81–84
integration of negative experience, 11–12
in relational field, 58
ritual process, 52–53
self-sponsorship practices, 54
chakra centers, 85

change
acceptance of uniquely deviant self, 24–26
cycles of, 46
help-seeking and, 27
as integration of fressen energy and essen forms, 20–21
as learning, 31
rationale for breathing awareness, 75
reconnection to relational field for, 22–24
relational connections for, 63–64
rituals for, 192–93
self-demands for, 25
self-relations conceptualization, 148–49
suffering and, 54
through sponsorship, 97
transformation of archetype, 161, 164
via self-relations, 42–43
Chodron, P., 119
Chopra, D., 94
cognitive self
activating and locating, 136–38
alienation of, 152
centering, 10
development of, 14–15, 27, 64
dissociation in consumerism, 40
as flowing experience, 9–10
functions of, 60
in healthy learning, 65–66
inflation of, 150
intensity assessment, 144–45
intensity of connectedness, 145–46
as mediator of relational differences, 60–62
nature of, 60
problem-defined, 67
relational buffers, 60
therapeutic significance, 21
collective consciousness, 14, 152–53
communion, experience of, 155
community
reincorporation of self into, postritual, 193–94
competency-based self
therapeutic focus, 112–13
therapeutic goals, 18–19, 67–68
complementary identity
accessing, 99
effective practice, 103
joining with presenting self, 100–103
therapeutic focus, 112–14
consumerism
conceptualization of love in, 41
dissociation of self in, 40
fundamentalism and, 41–42
as holding too loosely to life, 37, 40–41